# CONCILIUM

*Religion in the Seventies*

# CONCILIUM

*Concilium* 7, 1977: Canon Law

# JUDGMENT IN THE CHURCH

Edited by
## William Bassett and
## Peter Huizing

A CROSSROAD BOOK
The Seabury Press • New York

1977
The Seabury Press
815 Second Avenue
New York, N.Y. 10017

Library of Congress Catalog Card Number: 77-93986
ISBN: 0-8164-0365-1
ISBN: 0-8164-2166-8 (pbk.)
Printed in the United States of America

262·935

# CONTENTS

# Editorial: The Ministry of Those Who Judge

JUDGMENT in the Church is a silent and unheralded ministry. The confessor mediates the mercy of God in an individual encounter in which spiritual direction is given and forgiveness imparted in the strictest confidence. The bishop admonishes one of his priests on the basis of an informed conscience. There are no witnesses, there is no record; no opinion will be published to inform the community of the faithful. A marriage case is decided by the judges of a diocesan tribunal. Again, only the parties are informed of the decision. The record of the case is sealed for filing in the archives. A religious superior evaluates the record of formation to give words of welcome and reassurance as she admits a young sister to vows. In each case the labour of the men and women who are judges in the Church is shielded from review. Unlike the preacher, the liturgist, the organizer or the great administrator, the judge in the Church struggles with his task out of sight, alone with God.

This volume in the canon law series is dedicated to those who exercise the ministry of judgment in the Church. Some perform their ministry in the highly-formalized context of the judicial procedures of the church courts. The courtrooms of the Holy Roman Rota and the Apostolic Signatura in Rome echo appeals from lower courts arranged in hierarchical tiers through the metropolitan sees and into diocesan tribunals spread throughout the Catholic world. Few of the faithful have seen the operation of these courts; most hardly know of their existence. The pastor who is also a synodal judge, or an advocate, or defender of the bond in the diocesan tribunal is engaged in a kind of pastoral ministry in the diocese that few of his own parishioners are even aware of. Yet this is an ancient and indispensable ministry in the Church. The church courts are the oldest in the western legal tradition. In the Middle Ages their decisions inspired the humanistic principles of personal right and dignity that form the backbone of the civil law. Now the courts are hushed. They decide without civil sanction. Their rôle is voluntary and their decisions bear only upon the spiritual welfare of those who come to them for their help.

Most judgment in the Church, however, is informal. The tribunals touch the lives of relatively few persons. The sacramental life of the Church affects all the faithful. Each of the sacraments is an event in the Christian life that seals a relationship with Christ and the Church. It is a grace-filled event, an initiation, a confirmation, a stage of Christian growth, a step into ministry, a eucharistic meeting. Each sacrament builds up the Church and is consciously surrounded by a ministry of preparation, evaluation and conferral. This is a ministry of judgment in which the Church's canon law is read anew and interpreted millions of times daily for the direction of the liturgical and sacramental lives of men and women everywhere.

To admonish and forgive, to entreat and exhort are all the exercise of judgment. How should the judge conceive his ministry in the light of the Gospel and human prudence? This is a complex and difficult question. A new and extraordinary approach to the ministry of judges in the Church must be projected in the current efforts to reform and renew the canon law. The studies that have been prepared for this volume are a contribution to this endeavour.

A public judgment in individual cases, be it formal or informal, is a rare phenomenon these days. Occasionally one reads a press report of a sensational marriage case or of a struggle in a diocese issuing in bitter fulminations of excommunication and reprisal. Occasionally a book or a doctrine is publicly adjudged dangerous or contrary to the faith of the Church. Only on the rarest occasions is a person brought to public judgment in the Church. What would be the purpose? Few are any longer intimidated by such a judgment. In fact, we are uncomfortable at the thought. Shades of the Inquisition!

On the other hand, the experience of the Church since the closing of the Council reveals that the secrecy of judgment and the confidentiality of records are not unmixed blessings. There are injustices in the Church that simply cannot be redressed without access to a ministry of judgment that gives the possibility of a public vindication of the maligned and the aggrieved. Rights in the Church are meaningless without remedies. If I am denied the sacraments because of an unfounded rumour cast upon my good name, should the Church not give me a forum to clear my reputation? If I am harassed as a teacher by a pastor who is theologically benighted, should I not be given a hearing on my competency? If my children are dogged out of the parish school by a neurotic principal or headmaster, is this not a sufficiently serious matter to warrant my recourse to a properly constituted impartial board of arbitration? Fairness in the Church today demands that all the faithful have access to a ministry of judgment in the Church that will secure open justice.

In the aftermath of *Humanae vitae* hundreds of men and women were summarily dismissed from teaching positions in universities, seminaries, houses of religious formation, parochial and catechetical centres in all parts of the Catholic world. The birth control controversy precipitated the greatest purge of Catholic educational institutions since the Modernist crisis at the turn of the century. In some countries the public outcry was quickly muted. In others picket lines and wildly strident confrontations in the press secured some positions, hurt others and shocked just about everyone. *Humanae vitae* quickly passed from controversy to catalyst, revealing not only profound rifts among moral theologians but also deep, glaring inadequacies in the Church's laws and systems of justice. In effect, it quickly became obvious that the Church had no way of dealing with dissent on a massive scale short of compromise or complete ostracization. More importantly, for individuals whose lives and careers were caught in the morass there was nowhere to turn in the Church for protection of their basic rights.

Charges leveled against the dissenters ranged from allegations of heresy to betrayal of the Holy See and unfitness to teach. While some of the accused found strength in numbers, many were isolated and lost their livelihoods and professional esteem in the Church without appeal. Where are they now? Of nineteen members of the theological faculties at the Catholic University of America only three remain today. Others have gone to other institutions or have ceased teaching altogether. Follow-up studies elsewhere reveal a drift away from the Church that is of alarming proportions. The principal cause of the drift among professional scholars is not the dissent itself. It is, rather, a failure of confidence in the Church. For in time of crisis judgment was passed arbitrarily, without standards and without benefit of an impartial forum of appeal. In short, *Humanae vitae* revealed the ease with which sanctions can be meted out and the entire system of church courts and judicial processes can be closed off against those who dissent.

The bitter pill continues to convulse the Church deep in its inner life. If it is possible now to reconcile the official teaching of the Church with the practical imperatives of a living faith commitment at variance with it, we must wonder what will happen to those whose cries of conscience made reconciliation possible for the millions who kept their silence. Will there be an amnesty, a policy of reinstatement and understanding? Unlikely. In this long decade not one single case has come to public judgment in the Church. No one has been vindicated; no truth, no institution, no principle has officially been sanctioned. Judgment was driven underground in the birth control affair. There, out of sight, compromise and tergiversation allow life to continue, but leave the stigma of unfitness uneradicated. This stigma will tarnish the lives of those who could not or would not accept a teaching which the hierarchy has since admitted to be noninfallible, and which at the time was expressed as a tenet of the law of nature: something that educated people should know from their own reflective sharing in the human experience.

Is it a greater stumbling block to Christian people to hear of dissent and diversity of theological opinion or to see the dissenter pilloried and chastized without possibility of defence, or explanation of his motives, or even an impartial hearing upon the issue of his own right and his own conscience? In our day, the answer would have to be the latter. The Church should be a model of justice in the expectation of its people.

The post-conciliar age is marked by theological and institutional conflict. Conflict is rarely abstract; rarely a matter of conceptual differences of opinion. It involves persons. Frequently the results of conflict are alienation and lasting injury. In the Church conflict sets person against person in the most profound crisis of identity, for both believe the Church to be in fact a community of grace, of understanding, reconciliation and justice. Where conflict becomes debilitating and lives are injured, both struggle to find a forum in which justice may be served, the value of articulated insight protected and the innocent set free. The real Church, however, in fact provides no such forum. Appeals to Rome for its favour are a poor surrogate. The avenues of redress for the injured and accused are meagre indeed.

There is, indeed, a problem of justice and judgment in the Church. The reform of the canon law cannot proceed in oblivion of this concern. The studies in this volume were written in the belief that the Church can take initiatives now to become for all its members a community in which justice lives as a preciously guarded, yet procedurally accessible, ideal.

This volume has not been spun out of the fantasy of dreamers. It was conceived by lawyers of wide experience in canon and civil law; by men and women whose life experience in the Church involves the day-by-day realities, the actual and the possible. They know what the problem of justice and judgment involves practically. Diocesan tribunals are clogged with marriage cases, but unable or unwilling to hear appeals from administrative grievances. Theologians are still cast under suspicion, and investigated and blackballed without notice or recourse. Teachers in Catholic schools are denied the basic right to collective representation. Arbitration and reconciliation procedures are available only after threats of extortionary and scandalous publicity. The laity may be hobbled in virtually any relationship they have with the sacramental and institutional life of the Church in parishes and schools, and the bishop will invariably support a tenured pastor. The Church in its practical life remains a paternalistic institution in which justice is meted out by favour. Glorification of the internal harmony and consistency of the system of canon law does not solve the practical problems in which law and life converge in conflict. Acquiescence to injustice on the plea that we have no law to cover the matter is a perversion of the ministry of judgment. The failure to give access to impartial judgment is itself to judge.

The church courts, as part of a universal and ancient legal system, are clearly the focal point of stress in a time of reform and growth in the law. Though a growing volume of literature in nearly every language area continues to catalogue the failures of the courts, there is a consensus that a good, working system of agencies of conflict-resolution in the Church would be of immense service to the faithful. The canon says that it is desirable that all quarrels among the faithful be avoided (Canon 1925:1). This, however, is unreal. *Habent sua sidera lites*. The suppression of conflict by refusal to acknowledge its existence or by a conspiracy of silence in the hope that time will blanket memory is wrong. It involve the sacrifice of truth and right to a norm of expediency. This would mean the total submergence of the interests of the person in a selfish and superficial community whose external tranquillity would become the measure of right. Clearly, there must be ways in which conflict can be resolved. In an age of instantaneous communication and the educated participation of the laity in the processes of direction of church life these ways of conflict resolution will have to entail also the fullest measure of disclosure and reasoned judgment.

Several initiatives in the Church give foundation to a real optimism that the major problems of justice are recognized and that efforts are being made to solve them. In an official way the Commission for the Reform of the Code of Canon Law has already taken steps to institute procedures in newly-formed administrative tribunals in various countries that will permit the orderly resolution of many kinds of administrative conflicts. New procedures for hearing marriage cases and deciding them more expeditiously have been adopted. Some churches have already promulgated guidelines and set up agencies of arbitration and reconciliation. A new phenomenon of published court decisions, similar to civil law reporting systems, facilitates the communication of ideas and the evolution of a living jurisprudence in the Church. A declericalization of the staff of chanceries and tribunals is proceeding elsewhere, particularly in the mission churches. Reports and comments on these initiatives also form part of this volume.

The reform of canon law is but one factor in a perceptible series of changes that is gradually transforming the Church in our own generation. A new theological awareness corresponds to the renewal of the liturgy and the revitalization of mission. Not all changes are good or will leave a lasting impression on the Church. Some, however, will. In the process of experimentation and testing they will be refined and become a permanent and valued part of the structures of the Church for ages to come. We believe that this age of extraordinary sensitivity to justice will leave the Church just such a contribution in improved ministries of judgment to secure justice for all.

The first part of this issue is dedicated to an historical analysis of the development of the formal judicial system of the Church on a diocesan level and the restrictions that were put upon its competency by the reforms of the Council of Trent. Elizabeth Schüssler-Fiorenza deals with the New Testament communities, and the exercise of corrective and disciplinary judgment within them, in order to explore the contemporary hermeneutical problem of using the New Testament church as a paradigm for later developments. Hartmut Zapp traces the role of bishop as judge in the Church, and the ancient canonical forum, the *audientia episcopalis,* as forerunner of the diocescan synod and the modern tribunal. Pier Giovanni Caron answers from a post-Tridentine perspective the most perplexing of questions relating to a judge in the Church: how did the healing office of reconciliation and mercy turn into a role of legal interpretation and the enforcement of ecclesiastical law.

The second part of the issue concerns the major problems of reform in the office of judge in the Church. The judge in the diocese is a mediator of justice and a protector of individual rights, in the words of Juan Luis Acebal. His ministry is one of truth. Jean Bernhard explores the implications of a new dimension of ministry in the Church by suggesting structures of judgment that draw from the competencies of religious and laity as well as the clergy. Thomas Green writes of cooperation among the judges, a sharing of insights to create in the Church a new, living science of law, a new jurisprudence to assimilate in the context of faith the ongoing experience of the faithful.

Two chapters are devoted to actual developments that are currently interwoven into the reform of canon law. Hans Heimerl gives details of initiatives to provide procedures of arbitration and reconciliation in various parts of the Church. Francis Morrissey summarizes the procedural and administrative reforms that have already been put into practice in the post-conciliar structures of the Church.

The final section of the issue is devoted to three reflective studies bearing upon fundamental principles of the ministry of judges in the Church. We speak of judicial impartiality ordinarily in the context of conflicts of interest or subject bias. There is another dimension to impartiality that needs to be accepted as a precondition to the restoration of confidence in the ministry of judges. That is a non-ideological rôle. We must ask whether the judge is properly a resolver of disputes, or a policeman for the interests of the institutional Church. Are these rôles separable? What may be the implications of the separation? Enda McDonagh then breaches one of the most lively topics debated among moral theologians today: what is the meaning of scandal in this complex age of kaleidoscopic needs and expectations of the Church? The principal studies then conclude with a theological reflection upon the ministry and structures of judgment in the Church by John Noonan.

The volume is rounded out by a case study of the most famous of the post-conciliar conflicts, the case of the Washington Nineteen. It is a report of the frustration and anguish that followed *Humanae vitae* in the Archdiocese of Washington. It details the extraordinary efforts that were made by parties on both sides of the conflict to achieve a healing. Most of all, it reveals the inadequacies of the Church's present structures of judgment and makes practical the call for reform to make the rôle of judge in the Church truly the protector of human rights.

We end with words of dedication to the men and women of the Church who are judges in the traditional ministries or will become judges in rôles yet to be created, in an eloquent thought from the posthumous writings of the great judge of the Holy Roman Rota, Cardinal André Jullien: 'To every judge, and therefore to you, judges of the Church, God says: Love justice, all you who judge the earth" (Wis. 1:1) . . . we must pray through Jesus Christ that we may follow the strait and narrow way of justice, so that in our judgments our human justice shares in the divine Wisdom and eternal justice'.

*William W. Bassett*
*Peter J.M. Huizing*

Elisabeth Schüssler-Fiorenza

# Judging and Judgment in the New Testament Communities

IF we try to trace the establishment of canon law back to the New Testament, we immediately meet with methodological and hermeneutical difficulties. The *methodological* problem becomes immediately apparent if we compare the New Testament writings with those found at Qumran. In contrast to the latter, the canonical collection of early Christian literature does not contain a single document that could be classified as a rule or regulation concerning the Christian community. A few of the writings of the New Testament do contain directives which could be interpreted as legislative regulations or maxims. But no single NT code of regulations or codified constitution has been handed down to us.

How such a code of regulations might have appeared can be seen from that found at Qumran (1QS). The eleven columns of 1QS have been preserved virtually intact. However, the indications are that it does not form a literary entity, but is in fact composed of various traditional fragments. At the beginning there is a section with liturgical directions for the initiation of new members into the community. This section also contains directives for the annual celebration of the Feast of the Covenant (I,1–III,12). Learned instructions about the 'spirits of truth and wickedness' (III,13–IV,26) are followed by rules for the organization of the church and a comprehensive penal code (V,1–IX,24). The book closes with a psalm of praise and thanksgiving for God's justice (IX,24–XI,22). The church community is organized strictly according to rank and class. We find, for example, detailed directives of a disciplinary nature, principles for the admission and rejection of members, rules for the convocation of the general assembly and for the celebration of the Eucharist. Interpreters of both the NT and the writings of Qumran have pointed out similarities and parallels between certain NT directives and those given in the Qumran writings. Nevertheless, the fact remains that the NT does not contain a separate code book and that individual directives are incorporated in the parables scattered throughout the gospels and epistles. The question as to the foundation of canon law in the NT is thus primarily a literary problem.

The *hermeneutical* discussion of the problem and the relevant texts is largely characterized by a series of alternatives. Hence charisma or institution, spirit or ministry, love or law, community or official are presented as mutually exclusive alternatives.[1] Questions concerning the ministry and canon law seem to be indissolubly linked. This approach was greatly influenced by Rudolf Sohm's *Kirchenrecht* (Canon Law) which appeared in 1892. According to Sohm, the Church, being a charismatic community, cannot be a juridical organization. In the last analysis, organization within the Church stems from the one decisive source, the Word of God. The nature of the Church makes any kind of canon law an impossibility. The opposite view was taken by Adolf von Harnack who proposed a dual organization of faithful and ministers within the Church. In his opinion the law does not contradict the charismatic structure of the Church. The form, structure or constitution of the Church, imperfect though it may be, is essential.

In the debate between Harnack and Sohm, K. Holl put forward a compromise solution. He distinguished between the legal concept of the Church (the early Church in Jerusalem) and the charismatic (Paul and his communities). Preaching the Word is seen as a charism which introduces the element of righteousness, and so necessitates an ecclesiastical constitution. Ministry and charism are not identical yet the institution and laws are the ecclesiological consequence of certain charismata. Charism is always linked with tradition and the Church. R. Bultmann agrees with Sohm that legislation is always contrary to the nature of the Church if the tenets involved no longer serve as guidelines, but instead assume a constitutional character. On the other hand, he disagrees with Sohm's proposition asserting that the NT could not have come into being at all if charismatic doctrine and institutionalized tradition had been fundamentally contradictory. But since the preaching of the Word, which he sees as the central purpose of the Church, was not initially linked with an organized ministry of any kind, the early Church possessed neither ministry nor constitution.[2]

E. Käsemann has rightly observed that this line of argument is based on applying modern logic to the text of the NT and hence cannot lead to any valid conclusions. On the strength of critical analysis[3] of the texts he maintains that organization was introduced into the Christian community by means of the Spirit. The Spirit and the law are not mutually exclusive. Through his authoritative proclamation of 'doctrines of divine law' the early Christian prophet anticipated the Last Judgment and proclaimed God's law within the community of the Church. However, Käsemann draws a distinction between this divine or 'charismatic' law and canon or church law, and emphasizes that Christianity in its original form had no laws relating to the community, administration, discipline or the sacraments. Hence Käsemann's proposition ends up caught between the two premises of the Sohm-Harnack debate. Further studies in the history of form have also resulted in the exegetical basis of Käsemann's solution being questioned. The so-called 'tenets of divine law' in the New Testament are really words of wisdom in parable form and for the most part are not in fact legal principles. These studies have also shown that it was not the task of the early Christian missionaries to proclaim laws, but to prepare the Christians with warning exhortations and words of comfort for the Last Judgment.[4] From this it is clear that given the nature of the theological sources handed down to us, it is impossible to find direct evidence for the establishment of canon law in the NT. The NT contains no legal statutes or explicit regulations concerning the ministry, nor any timeless, universally valid principles. On the contrary, it gives us historically-conditioned directives and examples addressed to communities which at the time had virtually no organization or structure. Does this mean, then, that the NT is not relevant to the contemporary reform and restructuring of canon law?

This puts the hermeneutical problem on a different level. The aim is not so much to determine the relationship between charism and ministry or love and law with the help of the NT texts; but rather to ascertain by methodological means the relationship between historical interpretation and canonical discipline.[5] The study of canon law is generally concerned with the contemporary Church and its problems and turns to the Bible and exegesis in its search for Christian principles and standards. The historic-critical method of Biblical interpretation, on the other hand, brings out the specific historical character and the historically and culturally conditioned nature of the NT writings, thus emphasizing how remote the Scriptures are to contemporary problems. Despite these differences in method and purpose, the discipline of canon law remains one of the theological disciplines devoted to the revelation of the Scriptures. Similarly, NT exegesis as a theological discipline is concerned with the contemporary church. This raises the question as to how historically and culturally determined texts can have any meaning or theological significance for contemporary theology without losing their historical character and being transformed into universal principles.

This methodological rift between canon law and exegesis reveals a change of paradigm. The category of the paradigm evolved in the course of debates in the natural sciences. According to Thomas S. Kuhn,[6] a paradigm is a basic example of any given scientific tradition whose propositions and models are upheld and agreed to by all scientists in the field. Students do not acquire scientific methods of learning by formulated principles, but by means of concrete examples offering a variety of different solutions to a problem. The student learns to recognize similar situations and to use this knowledge to analyze and evaluate new situations. The Scriptures do not offer the canon lawyer any revealed propositions or principles. They are simply an account of historical events in historically conditioned language. Therefore, the canon lawyer has no option but to relinquish the scientific paradigms of his own tradition of research, with its basis of rules, laws and principles, and to come closer to the historically conditioned paradigm of the Scriptures. In other words, following the pastoral example of the Scriptures, canon law must develop into a pastoral, theological and historical discipline if it wishes to do justice to the theoretical paradigm of the NT. Only by calling to mind and reconstructing the example of the NT can we do justice to the historical revelation which is the essence of the Scriptures. This can never be achieved by any attempt to establish specific theological laws.

The aim of the following discussion of certain NT texts is to point out some important factors and perspectives concerning the reconstruction of a NT prototype for canon law. It will not be possible to examine every aspect of the texts, nor do I have the necessary space to discuss *all* the NT texts involved. Nor should the results be mistaken for actual NT dogmas. But the category of the paradigmatic, historical example gives me the possibility of drawing the texts out of their historical isolation and considering them in the context of a NT prototype for canon law.

## II

Linguistic investigations have shown that NT allusions to judging and judgment are mostly connected with God's eschatological judgment of mankind.[7] Justice and righteousness emanate from God and Christ. For this reason human beings are explicitly forbidden to pass judgment on their fellow men. The outright prohibition of personal judgment found in QS (Mt 7:1–2; par. Lk 6:37), as well as in St. Paul's epistles (Rm 2:1; 14:4, 10, 12; 1 Cor 4:5) and in the epistle of James (2:4, 12f; 4:11) probably stemmed originally from Jesus himself. Not only 'is there no Jewish analogy to this tradition, but it contradicts the general tendency of Jewish theory and practice. By means of this ban Jesus proclaimed the rights of the individual in the most explicit possible way. No-one has the right to judge his fellow-men . . .'[8] Each and every one of us is subject solely to God's jurisdiction. God will judge the individual according to how he judges his fellow men.

In Matthew the basic statement forbidding judgment is followed by the image of the speck in the eye of the judged and the log in the eye of the one who has passed judgment on him. In Luke it is linked to a didactic poem demanding that men treat their brothers with the same mercy and compassion that God shows towards mankind. However, in Luke the metaphor of the 'speck and log' is contained in a parable relating to just leadership within the community. The community of the disciples is a brotherly one. Its leaders run the risk of being accused of hypocrisy if they pronounce judgment on the insignificant misdemeanours of their fellow Christians but refuse to acknowledge their own far graver errors. The ominous authoritative warning in the metaphor of the 'speck and log' forbids the leaders of the community on principle to judge their fellow Christians, since they themselves always have a log in their own eye. Hence passing judgment is forbidden not only between individuals, but in the wider context of the community of the faithful.

In the same way Paul admonishes Christians in Rome not to judge or despise each other (Rm 14:1–12, 13). No one has the right to pass judgment on other members of the community, for this would be an infringement of God's powers as head of the community and judge of the world. Anyone who is aware that at the last judgment he will have to answer for all his deeds will try to avoid passing judgment on others. Paul is emphatic: 'The Church condemns and prohibits its members to pass theological sentence on one another. Each should approach his brother with a generous, open mind.'[9] Those who possess critical ability should not employ it to condemn others, but to achieve their well-being.

However, in Cor 5:1–13[10] and 6:1–11, Paul seems to expect some kind of judicial activity in the community. 1 Cor 5:1–13 deals with a case of outright incest, for marriage between a man and his step-mother was forbidden in both Roman and Judaic law. Not only does Paul demand that the sinner be excluded from the community, but that they are 'to deliver this man to Satan for the destruction of the flesh', so that his spirit may be saved on the Lord's day of judgment. This holy curse is not to be understood as a judicial act, but as an act of contrition or penance. Such measures were necessary to prevent corruption within the community. Despite the ritualistic terminology and mode of expression, Paul is not concerned to establish a ritualistic purity within the community, since this would mean that members of the community would have to avoid all contact with sinners and unclean persons. Paul is far more concerned with the moral integrity of the individual members of the community and of the community as a whole. The text is critical of those powerful members of the Corinthian community to whom Paul refers several times as the letter as 'boastful' (1:29; 3:21; 4:7; 5:6). The community should not be proud of being able to permit public sinners in its midst because of its spiritual predestination. Paul warns the Corinthians that a little bit of 'bad leaven' can corrupt the whole community. It should, nevertheless, be noted that Paul not only sees the community as a 'forum' for his words of condemnation; he places the final responsibility for action in the hands of the whole community. In the last analysis, it is the community that counts.[11]

1 Cor 6:1–11[12] deals with the Christian integrity of the community and not with 'the first seeds of jurisdiction within the Church'.[13] In the first part of this passage Paul admonishes the Christians in Corinth for bringing their grievances before non-Christian judges. He considers this unworthy of them, for the Christians themselves are to be the final judges of the world. Paul does not follow this up by arguing that Christians are thereby entitled to pass judgment on each other or that the leaders of the community should judge the members. Instead, he suggests that some wise member of the community should mediate between the dissenting parties. The emphasis is on a mediator, not a judge. In the second part of the passage (vv. 7–11), however, Paul stresses that it would be better if disagreements in the community could be avoided altogether. It would be better for Christians to suffer wrong than to defraud or do an injustice towards other Christians. Whereas in v. 2 and v. 3 Paul demands that the promise of the last judgment should determine the life of the community and its relationship to the world, in v. 11 he emphasizes that the life of the Christians and their relationship to each other was to be resolved by the transformation brought about by baptism. The Christian is endowed with a new existence, beginning with baptism and ending with the Last Judgment and the Kingdom of God. He must bring this new existence to bear upon the community in practical terms. It should also affect the judicial relationship among Christians. According to Paul, this new outlook should find expression in the maintenance of peace within the community and in the precept that 'it is better to suffer injustice than to do wrong'.

Mt 18 seems to be especially important for the reconstruction of a paradigmatic NT model for the institution of canon law. Critical analysis of the text does not make it clear whether it refers to a 'communal institution' or whether it is a pastoral sermon.[14] There can be no doubt that Mt 18, both in terms of style and theological approach, was written by the author of the gospel of Matthew. The chapter can be divided into two main sections of which the second in particular deals with community life (18:15–35). At the beginning of this second section the author adopts a traditional, disciplinarian approach (18:15–20) prescribing the various stages to be undertaken in dealing with sinners, culminating with their expulsion from the community. Early in the history of the Judaeo-Christian Church in Palestine and Syria Christ's words in 18:15 were expanded into a definite legal procedure which has parallels in the Qumran writings (1QS V, 25–VI, 1; cf. too CD IX, 2–4). This rule seems to reflect the typical Jewish attitude to 'tax-collectors and Gentiles' and hence cannot be attributed to Jesus himself. The community rule probably originated in some small Judaeo-Christian communities whose general assembly exercised the right to excommunicate. Even before the tradition of Matthew's gospel this community rule was associated with the words of the risen Christ. The phrase to 'bind and loose' (Mt 18:18) is probably the oldest form of a saying of the risen Christ and is also found in Jn 20:23 and Mt 16:18.[15] The power to bind and to loose relates to the life and teaching of Christians and is given to all members of the community. Mt. 18:19, 20 refers to communal prayer and assembly. Since these verses stipulate that the community gather together 'in the name of Jesus', both Mt 18:20 and 1 Cor 5:4 presumably allude to the official assembly of the community. God is present among the community gathered together in the name of Jesus.

The author of the gospel of Matthew has adopted this early Christian community rule and implicitly criticizes it by the way in which he follows it in his text with a comment of Jesus' about the boundless forgiveness of the disciple (18:21–22) and the Christian's essential duty to forgive, illustrated by the parable of the 'unmerciful servant' (18:23–34). 18:35 summarizes the whole chapter and stresses the fact that the Christian's treatment of his guilty brother in a reflection of his own treatment at the Last Judgment. In this way the author of the gospel according to Matthew emphasizes that life in a Christian community cannot be organized by means of legal procedures and principles. The Christian 'community' cannot be organized by means of statute and discipline; what binds it together is the spirit of forgiveness and solidarity even towards the constant sinner, whether he be a Christian or not. Since God has pardoned their guilt, Christians must likewise forgive those who have sinned against them.

In conclusion, it must be said that interpretation of NT texts cannot yield any guidelines or precepts for Christian community life or for the solution of current conflicts within the Church. Yet our analysis of the NT has pointed to elements and perspectives in the paradigmatic model of the Scriptures which could be important for our understanding of 'church organization' today. These include such elements as: the prohibition of judging our fellow men; the command to show boundless, unconditional forgiveness, eschatological responsibility and solidarity; the moral integrity of the community; the community as a 'juridically' responsible body; and a critical, questioning attitude towards regulations and codes of behaviour. They should not be overlooked when constructing a new pastoral-theological paradigm of canon law as a theological discipline.

*Translated by Sarah Twohig*

## Notes

1. H. von Campenhausen, *Kirchliches Amt und geistliche Vollmacht in den ersten drei Jahrhunderten* (second ed., 1963), pp. 135–62; G. Hasenhüttl, *Charisma Ordnungsprinzip der Kirche* (Freiburg, 1969), pp. 308–17.

2. R. Bultmann, *Theologie des Neuen Testaments* fifth ed. (Tübingen, 1965), p. 456.

3. E. Käsemann, 'Sätze heiligen Rechtes im Neuen Testaments', in *Exegetische Versuche und Besinnungen* II (Göttingen, 1964), pp. 69–82.

4. K. Berger, 'Zu den sogenannten Sätzen heiligen Rechts', *New Testament Studies* 17 (1970), pp. 10ff; U. B. Müller, *Prophetie und Predigt im Neuen Testament* (Gütersloh, 1975).

5. Cf. J. Blank, in *Concilium* 3 (1967).

6. T. S. Kuhn, *The Structure of Scientific Revolutions* (Chicago, 1970), pp. 189–91; I. G. Barbour, *Myth, Models and Paradigms* (New York, 1974), pp. 92–112.

7. Cf. F. Büchsel, *Theologisches Wörterbuch zum NT* III (Stuttgart, 1959), pp. 936–55.

8. H. Braun, *Jesus* (Stuttgart and Berlin, 1969), pp. 123f.

9. E. Käsemann, *Der Brief an die Römer* (Göttingen, 1974), p. 353.

10. Cf. G. Forkman, *The Limits of the Religious Community* (Lund, 1972), pp. 139–51.

11. Contra H. Conzelmann, *Der erste Brief an die Korinther* (Göttingen, 1969), p. 117.

12. L. Vischer, *Die Auslegungsgeschichte von 1 Kor 6,1–11* (Tübingen, 1955), pp. 5–20.

13. Cf. H. Conzelmann, *op. cit.*, p. 125.

14. W. Pesch, *Matthäus der Seelsorger* (Stuttgart, 1966).

15. A. Vögtle, '*Ekklesiologische Auftragsworte des Auferstandenen*', in *Das Evangelium und die Evangelien* (Düsseldorf, 1971), p. 252.

Hartmut Zapp

# Diocesan Jurisdiction: An Historical Survey

EVEN in pre-Christian times jurisdiction was included in the sphere of religion. To serve the law is to serve God. The Germanic legal assembly, for example, was considered holy. In Christian thought the image above all of the medieval (ecclesiastical) judge is conceived in terms of God judging mankind on the final day of judgment.[1] The extent to which ecclesiastical jurisdiction has influenced the development of secular legislation can be deduced from the recent recognition that the German words 'Richten, Richter, Gericht', to judge, judge and court, even in their linguistic form originate from the ecclesiastical sphere of the episcopal *correctio*.[2]

From the beginning, the bishop's *pastoralis correctio* formed the focal point and aim of his endeavours in matters of faith and discipline. In some respects the discipline of penance scarcely differs from a criminal procedure. The earliest sources already testify to the jurisdiction of the Church, in some cases warning Christians, presumably in accordance with 1 Cor 6:1–7, not to bring their (civil) disputes before pagan judges. In Christian communities it is the bishops rather than lay persons who perform the office of judge. This is emphatically stated in the *Didascalin* which probably originated in the second half of the third century and was incorporated into the important canonical collection of *Constitutiones Apostolicae* in the fourth and fifth centuries.[3] The decisive factor in the judicial activity of bishops, for which precise and detailed directions are given in the *Didascalin*,[4] is the task of mercy and salvation which they are entrusted to carry out in the name of the just (and judging) God.[5] In the mid-third century Cyprian described the

9

ecclesiastical judge as *vicarius Christi*. In the fifth century oriental collection of canons, falsely attributed to the first Nicene Council, Cyprian
refers to a bishop as *vicarius Dei,* which he then illustrates with an
impressive account of a quarrel over an inheritance.[6] This makes it
clear that in addition to exercising his jurisdiction to maintain discipline
in the Church and in questions of dogma among his community, the
bishop's jurisdiction applies to civil matters. For even the *Didascalin*
clearly describes the bishop as lord of his diocese, ruling over clerics
and laity alike, not only in charge of ecclesiastical discipline and criminal procedures but also invested with civil powers of jurisdiction.

This brings us to one of the most interesting aspects of episcopal
jurisdiction in the early Church, the *espiscopalis audientia.* Although it
has been the subject of numerous investigations, there are still many
questions to be answered about this form of episcopal jurisdiction. The
western church's attitude towards this institution even differs from that
held in the Roman Empire.[7]

Of prime importance in the *episcopalis audientia* is the bishop's activity as an arbitrator for peace in accordance with the Christian principle
of *aequitas;* he should advise and admonish quarrelsome brothers,
whether clerics or members of the laity, and attempt to bring about a
peaceful settlement of the dispute.

This power as an arbitrator for peace must be ascribed to the *episcopalis audientia,* although it should be noted that the concept of
ecclesiastical jurisdiction cannot be summarized in such explicit terms.
This is because 'even theoretically it would be extremely difficult to
differentiate between decisions on matters of faith, church discipline,
lay discipline, in church affairs and in the secular, civil or penal
spheres.'[8] In any event, in practice the individual areas frequently
coincided. In addition, until the time of the Christian empire we know
very little about the procedures of episcopal jurisdiction, especially as
far as civil disputes were concerned. The *Didascalin* would seem to
suggest that Roman methods for conducting court cases were adopted,
either whole or in part. However one should not underestimate local
influence, particularly in the east.

Under Constantine the diocesan jurisdiction of the bishop in the form
of the *episcopalis audientia* reached a new stage. In the year 318 Constantine gave state recognition to episcopal jurisdiction in civil affairs
(*Cod. Theodos.* 1.27.1). Recent research tends to dismiss this development as being of little significance. Nevertheless Constantine's decree
must have increased the importance of the *episcopalis audientia;* for not
only was the settlement of a dispute mutually agreed to in the presence
of a bishop now recognized by the state: the sentence passed by the
bishop had to be carried out. Another constitution dating from 333

(*Const. Sirmond.* 1), which appears to establish the competence of the bishop to pass sentence in civil actions even against the will of one of the parties concerned, is disputed both in terms of content and authenticity. But it is certain that the constitution of 398 (*Cod. Justin.* 1.4.7) endorsed the demand for the consent of both parties to accept the ruling of the episcopal court; having presented a more convincing argument, it proceeds to repeat a series of commonplaces. It also gives the impression of wanting to introduce a clause whereby the church would be entitled to compel individuals to appear before an episcopal court. Another imperial legislation concerning the *episcopalis audientia* (*Cod. Theodos.* 1.27.2–*Cod. Justin.* 1.4.8) emphatically equates episcopal decisions with those of the state courts, though it does not actually include them within the jurisdiction of the state.

Probably of greater significance in the history of ecclesiastical jurisdiction is the attempt made from the fifth century on to widen the scope of ecclesiastical issues dealt with exclusively by the episcopal court (*negotia ecclesiastica*) and the general demand for a special, exclusively ecclesiastical judicial competency for the clergy (*privilegium fori*). Both these demands must be seen in the light of the gradual rise of differences between Church and State. Imperial legislation made every endeavour to restrain these attempts at expansion.[9] According to Justinian's law reforms the episcopal court retained sole competence to deal with matters of a purely spiritual and ecclesiastical nature. Another reform stipulated that the clergy could only be prosecuted by members of the laity before an episcopal court,[10] although in criminal cases the clergy could be sentenced by a secular court. It was in the Germanic nations that ecclesiastical jurisdiction first suffered the adverse effects resulting from competition with the secular courts. The Franco-Merovingian legislation in particular restricted the special legal competence of the clergy at least for a time, despite the fact that since the sixth century the laity had repeatedly been forbidden by the councils to prosecute the clergy before a secular court without the consent of the bishop.

From the eighth century onwards episcopal jurisdiction became increasingly important. In the first place judge of all spiritual matters in his diocese, the bishop became more and more influential in the sphere of civil and penal law. The reason for this was that, in Germany especially, the bishop had the right to convene a synod.[11] The *iudicium synodale,* or synodal court, grew out of the pastoral visits made by the bishop to his diocese to administer the sacrament of confirmation and to give religious instruction. The chief purpose of these episcopal investigations was the religious and moral life of the laity. Charlemagne expressly entrusted the bishops with the responsibility of pursuing and punishing cases of murder, adultery, immorality and 'everything offensive to God'. The synodal court became increasingly important owing to the bishop's position as imperial emissary and because it was supported by the state in exercising its jurisdiction. It competed with the secular court (administered by the counts) which it eventually superseded. The scope of its competence expanded continually, until after a short while almost all offences came under the jurisdiction of the bishop. The pastoral work of the clergy, the way they conducted their priestly duties and their private lives, their training, as well as church buildings and finances were all examined by the bishop at the synodal court. So too was the religious life of the faithful (e.g. observation of fast and feast days, attendance at church services, superstition) and virtually all criminal offences ranging from murder to unpaid tithes. The well-known synodal handbook compiled by Regino of Prüm (906 AD) contains ninety-six of these synodal questions for the clergy and eighty-nine for the laity. Unjustified failure to appear before the court was threatened with excommunication. Towards the end of the ninth century the bishop would call (usually seven) witnesses to facilitate his investigations, placing them under oath to inform him of all known offences. The oath, and before it the ordeal, played a very important role in the actual proceedings. It should be noted that the synodal court developed along slightly different lines in each diocese—in Germany too—corresponding to differing local conditions.

Gradually, synodal courts for clergy and laity were held separately. When dealing with the laity, the court continued to convene in the parish church, whereas issues concerning the clergy were referred to a diocesan synod or, more frequently, to the general chapter. This meant that synodal courts for clergy and laity were also held at different times. The population had to pay dues to the episcopal synod. Again and again synods had to remedy abuses and urge the bishops to keep their synodal courts as short as possible in order to limit the financial burden on the population.

In the eleventh century the synodal court underwent a major transformation. The archdeacon, who for a long time had played an important part in helping the bishop to administer the diocese, then appeared to take full charge of the synod, to begin with still 'the eye and arm' of the bishop, in other words his representative and delegated judge. In the course of time his office became more and more independent, and he was given his own, regular powers *(iurisdictio propria et ordinaria)*.[12] The archdeacon became the first instance of judicial power in diocesan jurisdiction. Only the nobility and the order of knights were still directly answerable to the spiritual jurisdiction of the bishop. Even serious offences committed by members of the clergy were in the first instance referred to the archdeacon. The jurisdiction of the archdeacon gradually began to rival that of the bishop so that, by the twelfth–thirteenth centuries the archdeacon had encroached not merely on the bishop's position as judge. The jurisdiction of the archdeacon was sometimes so powerful that appeals were no longer made to the episcopal court, but directly to the archbishop or even to the Pope. However, it should be remembered that the jurisdiction of the archdeacon did not reach this degree of autonomy everywhere. On the contrary, considerable local differences can be discerned, also in Germany.

At the height of the archdeacon's power within the diocese an institution of episcopal jurisdiction was created which once again restored the bishop to his position as sovereign lord of his diocese. This was the official *(officialis)*, a designation which appeared towards the end of the twelfth century and to begin with had another meaning. By the middle of the thirteenth century, the term was narrowed down to signify the jurisdiction of a bishop, first of all in France and shortly afterwards in Germany and England. The widely held notion that the introduction of officials was largely due to the bishop's struggle against the archdeacons must be considerably modified in the light of recent discoveries. Nevertheless, the independence of the archdeacons did force the bishops to find new representatives to assist them with administration. Hence the archdeacon was gradually replaced in the episcopal curia by the official and the vicar-general. Given the continually expanding competence of ecclesiastical jurisdiction, it was in the judicial capacity that the need for an episcopal representative was greatest. There was also an increasing number of cases referred by papal mandate for trial by the bishop. Alexander III (d. 1181) granted bishops the power to appoint their own judges expressly for such cases (*Liber Extra* 1.29.6). This led to the bishops, following the example of the judges delegated by the Pope, delegating judges for their own area of jurisdiction. To begin with they were only commissioned to deal with specific cases, but within a short time they were appointed on a permanent basis. The debate as to whether these episcopal officials were regular or just—permanently—delegated judges was brought to a close by Innocent IV in 1246 when he recognized the episcopal officials as regular judges *(iudex ordinarius)* (*Liber Sextus* 2.15.3). After that bishops and officials together formed the consistory. The official became the bishop's 'alter ego', exercising in his stead the jurisdiction of the diocese. Excluded were those judges appointed by rescript of delegation, in particular the *audientia litterarum contradictarum,* since they really belonged under papal jurisdiction.

In this brief outline of the development of the episcopal official—

some archdeacons then also appointed their own officials—we must emphasize that the genesis of this post differed considerably from place to place; nor did it arise at one specific time. This is conclusively proved by the large number of publications relating to the statutes governing officials.[13]

The most significant factor in the development of these ecclesiastical judges and in the general strengthening of episcopal jurisdiction was probably the canonical discipline which blossomed in the twelfth and thirteenth centuries. In the mid-twelfth century, following the precedent of the already powerful and influential law schools, the systematic approach of the *Decretum Gratiani* gave impetus to the development of canon law and in particular the scholarly law-suit. The decree in fact deals rather scantily with this material, so early depictions of legal cases rely heavily on legal literature *(ordo iudiciorum)* going back to Justinian law. The numerous legal decrees issued by the so-called lawyer-popes were compiled into the *Compilationes Antiquae* and the *Liber Extra,* and these paved the way for an independent canon law. The popes insisted that bishops should also adhere to the new church law in exercising jurisdiction over their dioceses *(Liber Extra* 2.2.9). By the thirteenth century this law had become so complicated that it could only be used in ecclesiastical courts by those who knew it in very great detail. The bishops, insufficiently experienced in canon law, were forced to appoint legal experts among their officials *(iurisperiti).* A new genre of canonical literature came into being so that diocesan lawyers could have access to whatever part of the scholarly law they needed. Starting with Tancred's subtle work *(Ordo iudicarius,* 1216) which dominates all academic legal studies, the attempt was made to translate the law into practical summaries or compendia. Significantly, such descriptions first appeared in France which was also where bishops had first appointed legal officials. By the end of the thirteenth century a great deal of explanatory legal literature is recorded, often going into local particulars. From that time on the standard work in scholastic law was Durantis' monumental *Speculum iudiciale* (1270–90). Intended particularly for the use of judges, it deals with all material covered up to that time, divided into four sections (persons involved in the proceedings, law-suits, criminal proceedings, and a collection of precedents).

The professional qualification of judge trained in canon law doubtless helped to give him a position of great influence and esteem. But the real reason for the deference accorded to the ecclesiastical judge was probably due to the fact that he was the representative of the spiritual law. As the good judge *(bonus iudex),* combining the *iustitia* with *misericordia* and *caritas,* he tried to 'bring about justice in the light of eternal salvation'.[14] In passing judgment he should direct his gaze on

God alone, as canon law repeatedly urged him to do (*Decretum Cratiani* D.45 c. 10; *Liber Extra* 1.31.13; 2.19.13; 5.1.17).[15] Canon law is on one level a human, temporal law with all the consequences that entails. But over and above that it participates in the Church's mission to serve the *salus animarum* above all. It is precisely the medieval canon lawyers who saw this as the fundamental problem for canon law and they emphasized the eternal spiritual well-being of man as the ultimate aim of their jurisprudence. One of the best known summas to the *Decretum Gratiani* (*Elegantius in iure diuino*, p. 1, c. 43) promises eternal life as the reward for following canon law. The chief difference between ecclesiastical and civil law is explicitly stated in the specific aim of canon law: the *salus animarum*. For this reason canon law always took precedence over civil law as far as salvation is concerned.[16] Ecclesiastical judges and courts thus also shared the superior position enjoyed by canon law because of its spiritual purpose. Even a critic like Marsilius of Padua (d. 1342) considered the pre-eminence of the ecclesiastical judge over the civil one beyond dispute,[17] especially since the pre-eminence of the spirit was a predominant criterion in forming the mental outlook of medieval man.

There are additional reasons for the preference given to ecclesiastical jurisdiction by the faithful in the Middle Ages. To start with, judgment passed by learned judges guaranteed the quickest and best possible decision. Civil jurisdiction, often much less qualified and only based on special law, was very much held back. Hence the inadequacy of civil jurisdiction served to establish the competence of the ecclesiastical court (*Liber Extra* 2.2.10). In addition, the form of proceedings, the proper legal principles and the successive stages of appeal were recognized advantages of diocesan jurisdiction. As a rule canon law was always used. Roman or special law was consulted only as a subsidiary, which often happened in civil disputes, and in the final instance—though this was more difficult—common or customary law. Another factor in the preference for ecclesiastical law which should not be under-estimated was its powers of execution. First and foremost, excommunication. It has rightly been pointed out that the spiritual penalty of excommunication or interdict punished medieval men more harshly than any secular penalty, although excommunication often involved secular sanctions too. Excommunication was used frequently in the fourteenth and especially in the fifteenth century not just as a punishment but as a means of coercion. Failure to obey a summons to appear before an ecclesiastical court was revenged in in this way and the culprit thereby forced to submit. Debtors were also frequently excommunicated so that 'debtors were prosecuted by preference in ecclesiastical courts'.[18]

Ecclesiastical jurisdiction gradually claimed competence for the majority of all possible legal proceedings. The competence of ecclesiastical courts in spiritual matters and all related issues was universally acknowledged. Nevertheless difficulties did exist between spiritual and secular courts owing to differences of opinion as to what constituted spiritual and what secular subjects for dispute.

On the basis of the *privilegium fori* all cases involving a member of the clergy were heard before an ecclesiastical court. As far as the clergy were concerned, the competence of the ecclesiastical judge was virtually undisputed. The principle that the clergy could not be sentenced by the laity (*Liber Extra* 2.1.8,10; 2.2.1,2), so insistently repeated by the popes of the twelfth and thirteenth centuries, corresponds to the medieval sense of rank, that a person could only be judged by his equal. But also in civil disputes an exclusively ecclesiastical court was claimed and demanded for the clergy (*Liber Extra* 2.2.9). The clergy were even forbidden to renounce the *privilegium fori* and present their case before a secular court (*Liber Extra* 2.2.12). A tendency can also be observed to extend this privilege to members of a priest's household. Among those whose rank *(rationae personarum)* placed them under the jurisdiction of the ecclesiastical courts were crusaders, merchants and travellers and especially those in need of protection *(personae miserabiles)* such as the poor, widows and orphans (*Liber Extra* 2.2.15; 5.40.26), at any rate when the secular courts neglected their cases.

Naturally enough ecclesiastical jurisdiction claimed competence in all matters concerned with faith. An exceptionally large part of these *causae spirituales* consisted of the specific judicial treatment of the church's marriage law which in the twelfth and thirteenth centuries acquired the legislative form that has determined it ever since. Hence the episcopal courts also judged all matters concerning marriage settlements and legitimacy. Likewise all other areas of dispute connected with spiritual matters came under the jurisdiction of the ecclesiastical courts. Such claims on the part of the ecclesiastical courts soon encountered energetic opposition from the secular authorities. The decisive factor for the expansion of ecclesiastical competence on such miscellaneous matters *(causae spiritualibus annexae)* was that all contracts confirmed by oath were considered to be under ecclesiastical jurisdiction (*Liber Extra* 2.1.13; *Liber Sextus* 2.2.3).

The famous decree *Novit* of Innocent III (*Liber Extra* 2.1.13) finally provided the ground for bringing most remaining disputes and all offences before the ecclesiastical court. According to this decree any issue involving a sin *(ratione peccati)* had to be tried by an ecclesiastical judge, for only the spiritual forum was in a position to judge sin. By this means all actions performed by a Christian came under the jurisdiction of the Church.

Under these conditions it was obvious that virtually all offences inevitably came under ecclesiastical jurisdiction. In keeping with the stipulations of the *ratione peccati* the sphere of competence of the ecclesiastical judge included not only lapses of faith or morality but also every conceivable crime (murder, bodily injury, offences against the property of another, usury, forgery, perjury, fraud, and so on). It is understandable that this virtual monopoly of ecclesiastical jurisdiction should have led to hefty rivalry with the secular authorities. Nevertheless, there was an amalgamation of ecclesiastical criminal procedures and secular means of coercion, characteristic of the period. In any event, bishops often had the power of a secular lord as well. At the request of the ecclesiastical court the 'secular arm of the law' frequently carried out the sentence (corporal punishment) and excommunication from the church generally followed secular ostracism. And since offences of a religious nature also endangered Christian society they were punished by the secular powers as well (heresy). Ecclesiastical courts were forbidden to carry out the death sentence (*Liber Extra* 3.50.5,9) but given that anyone found guilty was then referred to the secular court, their complicity in and responsibility for the execution of the death sentence cannot be denied. Both ecclesiastical and secular jurisdiction were equally involved in the aberrations of the corrupt courts of inquisition and the resulting witchcraft trials.

Excommunication and interdict were without any doubt the church's most serious means of sanction or coercion. Gradually, in the fifteenth century in particular, they were frequently misused, for instance to enforce measures taken by the ecclesiastical court or to extort financial demands of various kinds. The abuse of excommunication in France was strongly resisted in the fourteenth century with the result that the king himself reserved the right to make the final decision as to the justice and validity of excommunication. The person so convicted could appeal to the imperial court '*ab abusu iudicum ecclesiasticorum*'. Similar attempts to restrict ecclesiastical jurisdiction was made in Germany where grievances against them were exposed in increasing numbers. These complaints should not be underestimated in the part they played in ever-increasing demand for church reform. Ecclesiastical jurisdiction was eventually subject to more and more curtailment of its competence, not just by the Reformation, but also by the reorganization of the secular legal system and by growing opposition from state authorities.

The Council of Trent did not introduce any noteworthy changes in diocesan jurisdiction. Its significance for the abolition of archdeaconal jurisdiction and authority is greatly exaggerated. It would be more correct to say that it consolidated a development that had already made considerable progress.

Even in the period that followed the official continued to be *the* ecclesiastical judge in the diocese. As the permanently available representative of the bishop, he exercised the regular jurisdiction of the diocese. As a rule he was granted penal powers at the time of his appointment for this very purpose. His former commanding position declined with the gradual disappearance of ecclesiastical jurisdiction from the state system, an outcome of the growth of secularization. He now enjoys the esteem within the church accorded to a jurisdiction solely concerned with the spiritual life of the church and the faithful.

*Translated by Sarah Twohig*

## Notes

1. Cf., especially, F. Merzbacher, 'Das geschichtliche Bild des kirchlichen Richters': *Arch. f. Kath. Kirchenrecht* 129 (1960), pp. 369 ff.

2. Cf. G. Köbler, 'Richten—Richter—Gericht': *Zeitschr. d. Savigny Stift. Germ. Abt.* 87(1970), esp. pp. 105 ff.

3. II 37.2, ed. Funk (Paderborn 1905, reprinted Turin 1962), p. 124.

4. Cf. II 45 ff., ed. Funk, pp. 138 ff.; cf. P. Caspers, *Der Güte- und Schiedsgedanke im kirchlichen Zivilgerichtsverfahren* (Düsseldorf, 1954), pp. 14 ff.; U. Mosiek, 'Das altkirchliche Prozessrecht im Spiegel der Didaskalie': *Österr. Arch. f. Kirchenrecht* 16(1965), pp. 183 ff.

5. II 11–12, ed. Funk, pp. 46 ff.

6. Ch. 15, Mansi 2,1044; cf. G. Vismara, *Episcopalis audientia* (Milan, 1937), pp. 60 f.

7. Cf. W. Selb, 'Episcopalis audientia von der Zeit Konstantins bis zur Nov. XXXV Valentinians III.': *Zeitschr. d. Savigny Stift. Rom. Abt.* 84(1967), pp. 162 ff. (literature, state of research).

8. Selb, 'Episcopalis audientia', p. 169.

9. Nov. 35 Valentinian III, cf. Selb, 'Episcopalis audientia', p. 215.

10. Cf. Nov. Justin. 79; 83; 123. 8:21–3.

11. Even more decisive is A. M. Koeniger, *Die Senderichte in Deutschland* (Munich, 1907); cf. also W. Hellinger, 'Die Pfarrvisitation nach Regino von Prüm': *Zeitschr. d. Savigny Stift. Kan. Abt.* 48(1962), pp. 1 ff.; 49(1963), pp. 76 ff.

12. Cf. especially, also for the subsequent description, W. Trusen, 'Die gelehrte Gerichtsbarkeit der Kirche': *Handbuch der Quellen und Lit. der neueren europ. Privatrechtsgesch.*, ed. H. Coing, vol. I (Munich, 1973), pp. 467

ff. (literature, state of research); for the academic law-suit cf. K. W. Nörr, 'Die Literatur zum gemeinen Zivilprozess', *ibid.*, pp. 383 ff.

13. Cf. literature classified by country in Trusen, *Gerichtsbarkeit*, pp. 499 ff.; and for the statutes pertaining to officials see also A. Steins, 'Der ordentliche Zivilprozess nach den Offizialstatuten': *Zeitschr. d. Savigny Stift. Kan. Abt.* 59 (1973), pp. 192 ff (literature).

14. Merzbacher, 'Kirchlicher Richter', p. 383; cf. also for legal definition of the *bonus index* in C.3 q.7 c.4.

15. Cf. A. Jullien, *Juges et avocats des Tribunaux de l'Eglise* (Rome, 1970), pp. 225 ff.

16. Cf. Henricus de Segusia, *Commentaria ad X 1.4.11* (Venice, 1581), fol. 32 va: 'Ubicunque vertitur periculum animae, canones vincunt leges'; ad X 2.24.28, fol. 135 ra: 'Canon vero consideravit utilitatem animae, quae est corpori praeferenda'. Antonius de Butrio, *Commentaria ad X 2.26.5* (Venice 1502) fol. 107v: 'Canonicus finis intendit utilitatem animae, civilis utilitatem civilis societatis'.

17. Cf. *Marsilii de Padua Defensor Pacis*, dict. II, cap. III, para. 12, ed. Scholz (Hanover 1932) 156: 'Igitur iudex ecclesiasticus, episcopus seu sacerdos, maxime primus, superior est quocumque iudice seculari. Finis enim ad quem dirigit ecclesiasticus iudex est vita aeterna'.

18. J. Hashagen, 'Zur Charakteristik der geistlichen Gerichtsbarkeit vornehmlich im späteren Mittelalter': *Zeitschr. d. Savigny Stift. Kan. Abt.* 6(1916), p. 213.

Pier Giovanni Caron

# Canonical Equity

IF we trace the formation and historical development of the concept of *aequitas canonica*, we find three components: the Roman concept of *aequitas*, imbued with the pregnant sense of perfect justice; the patristic concept of *misericordia* or *caritas*, which softens the rigour of the law; and the Aristotelian concept of *epicheia*, or the non-applicability of the law in cases where its application would appear manifestly unjust.* The first two came together to produce the elaboration of the concept of *aequitas* as understood in the *ius vetus Ecclesiae*—the law of the first eleven centuries of Christianity—first expressed by the Fathers, and then in the canonical collections before Gratian, with greater stress in the latter (e.g., Yvo of Chartres) on the idea *aequitas-justitia*.

### CLASSICAL CANON LAW

In Gratian, rather than the concept of *aequitas*—which seldom appears in the *Dicta* with the recognizably clear sense of "Justice"—the commonest notion is that of *misericordia*. The first Decretists—Paucapalea, Bandinelli, Rufino—follow faithfully in the tracks of the master on this point. It is only later, in Stéphan of Tournai and Uguccione of Pisa, that one can find a clear development of the concept of *aequitas canonica* within the framework provided by Roman Law. Uguccione's rotund affirmation: *'Ius est aequitas'* [1] marks the high point of this first cycle in the evolution of the doctrine of canonical equity. The *Glossa Ordinaria* on the *Decretum* [2] compiled by John the Teuton,

---

* The first part of this article is based on a recent monograph of mine on the subject; cf. P. G. Caron, *'Aequitas' romana, 'misericordia' patristica ed 'epikeia' aristotelica nella dottrina dell' 'aequitas' canonica* (Milan, 1971).

20

with its significant additions by Bartolomeo of Brescia, though later than Uguccione, marks a return to the older position, namely the reaffirmation of the patristic concept of *aequitas* understood in the sense of *caritas* or *benignitas*.

The dawn of the decretalist period brought the introduction of the third component, the concept of *epikeia*, originally defined by Aristotle and taken up by Aquinas, in the sense of a correction of positive law in a case where this could not be applied, since its application would result in an injustice.[3]

The most perfect synthesis of these three elements appears in the admirable *Summa Aurea*[4] of Enrico of Susa, Cardinal of Ostia. His doctrine contains a highly significant definition, which he claims to have borrowed from St Cyprian: '*Aequitas est iustitia dulcore misericordiae temperata*'. This brings together two meanings of the word *aequitas*, that of *iustitia* and that of *misericordia*. Later illustrations of this doctrine clearly show the concept that Susa felt should take precedence over applying the law: namely the idea that if application of the law appears manifestly unjust in a particular case, the case should be withdrawn without further ado from the sphere of the law. This is clearly very close to the notion of *epicheia* put forward by Aristotle and the Scholastics. This concept is already present in the classification worked out by Bernardo of Parma in his gloss on the Decretal *Ex Parte* of Honorius III: a classification which places *aequitas scripta* in first place, *ius scriptum* in the second, and *aequitas non scripta* in the third. *Aequitas non scripta* is applicable only in those cases not provided for either in written equity or written law, or in which the legislator, where he sees they are provided for, considers the law non-applicable, since its observance would, under the circumstances, prove harmful to the common good. The exact correspondence between this notion of *aequitas non scripta* and the Aristotelian doctrine of *epikeia* adopted by St Thomas leads one to think that the Decretalists, contemporary with or slightly later than the Angelic Doctor, were familiar with the latter concept, which was not to receive its most complete expression till the works of Suárez some centuries later.

The concept of *epicheia* was originally, in Aristotle, that of an ethical and moral rule; but the recognition of the validity of its use by judges in the secular courts, made by St Thomas, enabled it to acquire a purely juridical meaning, namely that of 'ideal justice' or of 'justice to fit the particular case'. Suárez, the greatest interpreter of St Thomas' thought, later distinguished the various possible cases in which *epicheia* could be applied.[5] The first was the case of default of the authority of the legislator, who could not impose unjust sentences, and, when he did so, such sentences would be less binding, unless there was an appeal to the Prince to make them so. The second was that of lack of will on the part of the legislator himself, in which case it had to be supposed that this will, in this particular case, had not been expressed in all its clarity.

Equity comes in for consideration in Suárez's thought, then, under two different aspects. Under the first, equity, understood in its higher sense of perfect justice, is placed as guide and limitation to the power of the Prince in the event of manifest injustice in the law, unless there has been recourse to the Prince himself in order to obtain suspension of the efficacy of the law itself. Under the second aspect, however, *epikeia* takes on—in the interpretation of it in St Thomas' thought given by Suárez—the sense of *relaxatio legis in casu speciali, of dispensatio* or *benignitas*. In this way, the concept of *epikeia* comes to coincide in Suárez's thought—as it did earlier in St Thomas'—with that of *benignitas, or the patristic misericordia*.

In a case where the law should not be applied *propter iniquitatem,* the Angelic Doctor affirmed that there could be recourse to the legislator, in order that he might pronounce on the merits of the case, since only Princes *'propter huiusmodi casus habent auctoritatem in legibus dispensandi'*. But the word *dispensandi,* which led Suárez to identify *epikeia* with *dispensatio,* really means, in this passage of St Thomas, interpreting, following the legislator's mind, so as to ascertain which particular cases he had not meant to make reference to. *Epikeia* in St Thomas thereby comes to take on the value of a source of interpretation: this, given the Angelic Doctor's dictum of the duty to have recourse to the legislator, will be an authentic interpretation, because it will be up to the legislator himself to declare, *praetermissis verbis legis,* his *propria intentio.*

Furthermore, before Aquinas, the Decretists and the first Decretalists display efforts to make equity include the means of bringing out the true intentions of the *conditor legis.* So for example in Uguccione of Pisa, the rule of interpretation is that by which *aequitas* is identified with the *ius,* so that this must always be observed, while the *dispensatio* or *misericordia* does not have to be observed, *'nisi loco et tempore necessitatis vel utilitatis causa vel alia causa'*.[6] On the other hand, John the Teuton, in his *Glossa Ordinaria* on the *Decretum,* stated: *'Potius debet iudex sequi miseriocordiam quam rigorem'*.[7]

This direction prevailed originally in the decretalist doctrine. Bernardo of Parma, in his gloss on the decretal *Ex Parte,* recognizes, following the lawyers of the Bologna school, that *aequitas scripta* should take precedence over the *ius,* and that *aequitas non scripta* should prevail where there is no written law.[8] But this is not so much the *aequitas-iustitia* of the Glosses as the *iustitia dulce miseriocordiae temperata* spoken of by Enrico of Susa, Cardinal of Ostia, in this same golden age of Canon Law.

On the subject of interpretation of the law, he remains faithful to the principle of the pre-eminence of *misericordia* over *rigor*. This is not to identify *aequitas* with *misericordia*, since he retains Uguccione's *aequitas-ius* as permanently valid; but he does not insist, as the Pisan decretist had done, on the exceptional nature of *misericordia*. For Enrico, *aequitas, ius* itself, is justice tempered with mercy, and this is what the judge must always have *prae oculis*.

But the Cardinal of Ostia's concept of *aequitas = iustitia dulcore misericordiae temperata* is not a simple criterion of interpretation, of investigation into the mind of the legislator, suggesting that, when he has not been able to take a particular case to be judged into consideration, he should be more inclined to leniency than to a strict application of the letter of the law. It is a higher concept, something transcending the limitations of human understanding of the law, tending toward a higher *ratio*, of divine origin, toward the ideal, that is, of perfect justice. Such a concept, then, clearly shows a Christian amendment of the *ius vetus*. But this concept was destined to be superseded by one proposed by later canonists, following the Roman glosses, according to which *misercordia* came to be reserved to the role of simple exception.

The contradistinction between *aequitas* and *rigor* remained, nevertheless, the basis of the doctrine of the canonists who followed the Cardinal of Ostia. But, because the method of the commentators was to seek to extend the application of the letter of the law to the greatest number of cases, the result was that application of equity became somewhat restricted by virtue of this criterion.

The principle laid down by Accursio—that equity should be used only when it is written or when the law is silent on a point, while written law should prevail in all other cases—was adopted by Dino of Mugello and his pupil Cino of Pistoia (late thirteenth century to early fourteenth).[9] The latter, however, attenuates the strictness of this principle by stating that written equity can be used even when it contradicts *rigor scriptus*, if there is some doubt about the exact meaning of the latter.

After Cino of Pistoia, the last major contribution to the theory of the use of equity as a means of interpretation was made by the distinguished Doctor *in utroque jure* of the School of Perugia, Baldo of the Ubaldi.[10] In his teaching, the concepts of 'equity' and 'interpretation' coincide perfectly, in his affirmation that the law can no longer be applied when the end desired by the legislator is in default. It is noticeable that, in reaching this conclusion, the Perugian Master seems to be taking account of the scholastic notion of *epikeia*, which coincides, at least materially, with that of *aequitas* when the applicability of a law fails in a certain case in point, even though its literal formulation would seem to have included such a case.

The doctrine of *aequitas* elaborated by the medieval canonists reached its apogee with Baldo of the Ubaldi. Later, as the works of the commentators levelled off—in both Canon and Civil Law—into the no longer apt *mos italicus iuris docendi*, they did no more than transmit, more or less paraphrased, the conclusions the great jurists of the golden age had reached. Their works became a grey plateau of juridical research, limited to detailed commentary on what had already been said on every subject dealt with by earlier writers.

## POST-TRIDENTINE JUDICIARY PRACTICE AND THE ECLIPSE OF EQUITY

At this point it seems opportune to pause to examine what became of the principles relative to canonical *aequitas* in their application in judiciary practice, starting from the period from which better knowledge of such practice dates, a period which also marks the eclipse of the idea of equity, which gave way to a more rigouristic concept of discipline and of Church law in general: I refer to the period when the spirit of the Tridentine reform triumphed in the Roman Tribunals.

In the shining earlier period running from the beginning of the thirteenth century to the middle of the fifteenth, the triumph of the idea of equity in its highest sense had reached its high point in a sentence passed by the judges of Bologna: faced with the question of whether the death penalty, laid down in the civil statutes for anyone who spilt blood in the *Palazzo Communale,* should be applied to a surgeon-barber who had spilt blood there in order to save a sick man, they had replied that it should not. With this sentence, *aequitas* was raised to its highest dignity as a vehicle of interpretation; because the judges, searching for the *ratio legis* in the light of equity, had been able to conclude that in this case in point the aim of the legislator was in default, and to decide that the law was therefore inapplicable.

The post-Tridentine jurisprudence of the Roman Tribunals came to imply the eclipse of *aequitas* at the hands of the strict principles inspiring the Counter-Reformation. This was a reaction against the collapse of the universal monarchy of the Popes that had been going on over the previous centuries, a collapse that coincided with the end of the medieval world.

The universal Papacy, during the exile in Avignon, had become an instrument of French power politics; then, soon after the return of the Holy See to Rome, the unity of Christendom was torn apart in the storm of the Great Schism. Then the spiritual approach of the modern world opened up the road leading to Luther and Machiavelli, and so on to the trauma of the Protestant Reformation and the reaction against it embodied in Trent.

Study of the jurisprudence of the Rota in the sixteenth century shows how far this had become the expression of the rigoristic understanding of church law brought in by the Counter-Reformation. Not that the concept of equity had disappeared from its sentences: rather, contrary to what seems the general opinion, it had taken on a particular importance. But this concept of equity tended to aquire a strictly juridical character, becoming identified with 'perfect justice' and thereby losing the component of *caritas* or *benignitas* that, in particular cases, implied a *relaxatio legis*.

So, we find in a sentence from the Rota of this time (*Romana Retractus*, 29-I-1629, *coram Merlino*)[11] the statement that, '*rigor scriptus praeferri debet aequitati non scriptae';* and in another from the same period (*Mediolanem. Pecuniaria*, 18-VI-1629, *coram Motmanno*),[12] credit antedating a debt was not allowed to be taken *in contra* the amount of the debt, *ratione aequitatis.*

But the Rota judgment that best illustrates the limits placed on the application of equity in the Counter Reformation era is *Urbevetana Rescissionis Contractus* (24-I-1633, *coram Merlino*),[13] which was signalled out as '*magistralis decisio, et legale eruditione plena'.* This proclaimed the invalidity of a sale *propter conditionis defectum,* since the price of the article sold had not been laid down by the expert entrusted with estimating it. The ruling was that *aequitas canonica* could not be invoked to entrust deciding the value of the object in question to '*arbitrium boni viri'.* The reason given for not having recourse to such "equity" was that: '*haec equitas non reperitur scripta',* and therefore the rule by which '*iuris rigor servandus est ubicumque aequitas non est scripta'* was to be applied. The judge was not able to invoke at will an equity that ran counter to the written law. The dominant reasoning behind this and other similar judgments of the time was that equity counter to the dictates of the law could not be invoked, since equity was to be understood only as being in harmony *(congruentia)* with the principles of natural law.

## A NEW DIRECTION IN THE LIFE OF THE CHURCH

This tendency was to last to our own days in the jurisprudence of the Roman Tribunals; till, that is, the 'new direction' given to the life of the Church by the second Vatican Council. A foretaste of this 'new direction' was provided by the address of Pope Pius XII, on the occasion of the opening of the juridical year of the Roman Rota, on October 1, 1940; 'As a daughter of the Church, the sacred Roman Rota too must know how to combine justice with mercy, since mercy, justice's companion, is not ignorant of human weakness, timidity and malice; its concession of ample freedom to the defence and assistance to the poor does not obstruct the uncorrupt and impartial application of the law through jurisprudence'.

And another notable sign of the times—even though it does not originate in the Catholic Church—is to be found in the preliminary report to the recent Council of the Orthodox Church, in which *akribìa*, which seeks the strict application of Canon Law, is challenged in the name of *oikonomìa*, which is the modified and flexible application of this Law. This saving *oikonomìa* of the Church is set in the context of that of Christ. It is therefore the rule and duty of the Church, in accordance with the example of the *oikonomìa* of Christ, to watch over the various weaknesses and failings of men in the life of the Christian faith with this same love and tenderness, like a mother, through means of grace.

## AFTER VATICAN II

The new situation of the Church since Vatican II has brought the difficult problem of how to regard the sentence pronounced, in the name of *aequitas,* against or outside the law to the fore. At present, this question is even more difficult to resolve, since the revision of the code of canon law in the light of the new directives stemming from the Council is still in progress. While on one hand the urgent need for a more dynamic view of justice and a more functional interpretation of the law is undeniable—on the lines that man himself should be able to recognize what is morally just, not starting only from what is in conformity with the law—, on the other, it is equally true that the present code of canon law cannot be held to have lost its validity simply because it is in the course of being revised.

As a distinguished student of the new problems of church law, Lombardia, said, the mystery of the Church has a dimension of justice, and it is the canonists' task to uncover this, so as to show the harmony between the divine plan and the lines the Church has to follow in its human and contingent juridical dealings. This 'dimension of justice' implies that *aequitas* neither can nor should mean the obliteration of Canon Law. This law is strictly necessary to the life of the Church, and any appeal to *caritas* used as a pretext for evading fulfilment of one's own duties and respect for the rights of others is nothing more than sophistry.

The fact that the present *Codex* seems, in many respects, to have been outdated by current social realities—and indeed by the magisterium of the Church, particularly by the documents of Vatican II— should not be taken as pointing to the extreme conclusion that it should be abolished. It is with this in mind that we should consider the problem of the application of *aequitas* in the present stage reached by the evolution of church law: an application that must be made in the context of a juridical order always valid as such, and one seeking, as far as humanly possible, the attainment of perfect justice. *Epikeia* should have its place in those negative cases where it is permissible to choose individual freedom rather than the letter of the law. Beyond the legal requirements, *epikeia* can sometimes suggest, and even impose, compensation superior to that envisaged by positive law.

Paul VI, speaking on the occasion of the quincentenary of the promulgation of the *Codex*, expressedly stated that law in the Church cannot be regarded simply as an exercise of authority, but has to be seen as an instrument for safeguarding the freedom of the physical beings and moral bodies that comprise the Church. The Pope's message should be applied particularly to reform of the Roman Curia—especially in relation to safeguarding the rights of the faithful—and to the penal sphere, where a basic reform is needed in order to remove the complexity of the rules laid down in the present *Codex*, which render it unusable in practice. This reform must remove the possibility of anyone being tried without sufficient guarantee of defence and of receiving true justice; it must seek a way for the application of canonical sanctions to be based on a profound respect for the person of the accused, whose right to act in conformity with his conscience must always be safeguarded. But when a serious infarction that involves the community has been established, sanctions should be imposed not as a form of coercion of the law-breaker, but as a safeguard for Church order in relation to the community and for the integrity of Christian witness. Seen in this light, the idea of *aequitas* understood in its pregnant sense of perfect justice—and integrated with its component of Christian *caritas*—must play a vital part in the reform of the *Codex* and the application of its norms to particular cases. *Aequitas* will thereby transcend the strict letter of the law—which is still necessary, however, and which cannot be dispensed with in a perfect society, such as the Catholic Church aims to be—in order to realize the ideal of *caritas*, of divine love. To finish, it seems appropriate to recall the words of one of the choicest spirits of modern Catholicism, Jacques Maritain: 'The law is just. The law is necessary—necessary, that is, in the sense of preparing men for redemption: for eternal life with God. But the law is not God. And God is not the law—He is love.'

*Translated by Paul Burns*

## Notes

1. Hugutio Pisanus, *Summa super Decreto*, super D. L (Bibl. Vat., ms. Vat. lat. 2280, fol. 50 ra).

2. Joannes Teutonicus, *Glossa Ordinaria in Decretum*, ad c. 18, *Exigunt*, C. I, q. 7, gl. s.v. *causae*.

3. St. Thomas, *Summa Theologica*, I$^a$–II$^{ae}$, q. 96, art. 6; *ibid.*, II$^a$–II$^{ae}$, q. 120, art. 1.

4. Henricus A Segusio Cardinalis Hostiensis, *Summa Aurea* (Lugduni, 1568), lib. V, tit. *De dispensationibus*, n. 1, fol. 436 vb.

5. F. Suarez, *De legibus ac de Deo legislatore*, Lib. VI, Cap. VII, n. 11 (*Opera omnia*, ed. Berton, Paris, 1856, vol. VI).

6. Hugutio Pisanus, *op. cit.*, ad c. 25, *Ut constitueretur*, Dist. L (Bibl. Vat., ms. Vat. lat. 2280, fol. 50 ra).

7. Joannes Teutonicus, *loc.cit.*

8. Bernardus de Botono Parmensis, *Glossa Ordinaria in Decretales D. Gregorii Papae IX* (Venice, 1605), Lib. I, tit. 36, *De transactionibus*, c. 11, *Ex parte*, gl. s.v. *Aequitate*.

9. Dynus Mugellanus, *Commentarius mirabilis super titulo de regulis iuris* (Lyons, 1540), Regula 2, *Possessor*, fol. 19 verso; Cynus Pistoriensis, *In Codicem et aliquos titulos primi Pandectorum Tomi, id est, Digesti veteris doctissima Commentaria* (Frankfurt am Main, 1578; reprint Turin, 1964), Super Codic. Lib. I, tit. XIV, *De Legibus et Constitutionibus Principum*, I. 1, *Inter aequitatem*, c. 12, fol. 25.

10. Baldus Ubaldi Perusinus, *In primam Digesti veteris partem Commentaria* (Venice, 1599), tit. *De iustitia et iure*, 1. 7, *Omnes populi*, nn. 59–60, fol. 14 r.

11. *S. Rotae Romanae decisionum novissimarum a Paulo Rubeo J.C. Romano selectarum*, vol. I (Rome, Typis Vaticanis, 1642), decis. CCXLIII, coram R.P.D. Merlino Decano, *Romana Retractus*, 29-I-1629, n. 21, pag. 465.

12. *Ibid.*, decis. CCCV, coram R.P.D. Motmanno, *Mediolanensis Pecuniaria*, 18-VI-1629, n. 6, p. 575.

13. *Ibid.*, vol. II (Rome, Typis Vaticanis, 1640), decis. CLXXII, coram R.P.D. Merlino, *Urbevetana Rescissionis Contractus*, 24-I-1633, nn. 54–59, p. 327.

Juan Luis Acebal

# The Function of the Diocesan Judge

THE role or function of the diocesan judge, who exercises the judicial function in the name of the bishop, can be analyzed from three aspects: that of the rôle 'laid down' by the law (what his rôle should be); that of the 'real' rôle which he fulfils in practice (what the judicial rôle is in fact); and the 'ideal' rôle (what it would be desirable for the rôle of the diocesan judge to be).[1] Space does not admit of a full development of these three dimensions so I propose to synthesize some aspects of the rôle laid down and include some short considerations on the ideal rôle.

### DETERIORATION OF THE FUNCTION OF THE DIOCESAN JUDGE

Before analyzing his rôle it is well to make some observations on certain factors which have led to a diminishing of his prestige and his mission.

The function of the diocesan judge has been weakened in the first place through cases that law itself has withdrawn from his jurisdiction. There are in effect a whole series of cases that have been reserved to the Roman Pontiff or to the tribunals of the Holy See (Canon 1557) some of which could well be heard by the diocesan judge. Another class of litigation that has been placed outside his competence is that referring to the temporal goods of the bishop, the bishop's household or the diocesan curia. Disputes arising inside a religious institute of pontifical institution are likewise removed from his jurisdiction. He has no power to instruct in matrimonial cases of non-consummation and of dissolution in favour of the faith and the same applies to cases brought against holy orders, not to mention causes for beatification and canonisation.

29

There is now a new class of withdrawals that is going to reduce and weaken the prestige of the diocesan judge still further; these will stem from the institution of regional or multi-diocesan tribunals. Up to the present these have been 'special' tribunals; that is they are competent to hear matrimonial nullity cases but corresponding diocesan tribunals continue to exist in each diocese as 'general' tribunals, competent to hear every type of case except those of nullity. The Holy See supports the creation of these multidiocesan tribunals, which according to all indications will become far more common in the future. The most important aspect is that, as planned, the multi-diocesan tribunals will be able to handle any type of case, not only those of nullity. It has been said that existing regional tribunals in practice take over the judicial function of the diocesan bishop and therefore necessarily of his officials, but if in the future these tribunals acquire a general competence this suspension of his authority will be much more radical.

In practice this will mean that the competence and role of the diocesan judge will be reduced to those cases which can be dealt with through the foreseen summary procedure, and these in common law will only be cases of conjugal separation—cases which in virtually all countries, with the exception of Spain, are practically nonexistent today. If we add to this the well-known fact that diocesan tribunals are inactive bodies except for matrimonial cases we can form an idea of the serious deterioration that is likely to occur in the function of the diocesan judge in the future.

The creation of the proposed administrative tribunals will not improve his situation since administrative justice is not entrusted to the ordinary tribunals and their sphere will also be greater than that of one diocese: i.e., regional or national.

These structural and organisational forms make the outlook for the diocesan judge a very dark one since the multi-diocesan tribunal will take over many of his functions, and the basic limitations of the diocese as a unit of administration of justice will become more apparent. On the other hand the regional judge and the autonomous diocesan judge will come more into their own.

## THE MISSION OF THE DIOCESAN JUDGE IN GENERAL

The mission of the diocesan judge could be summed up by saying that his task is to make justice reign in the diocesan community by means of sentences that apply the laws with fairness to the case brought before him. In slightly greater detail, his function has the following generic objectives, either directly or indirectly: to safeguard the freedom, dignity and other rights of the faithful; to re-establish order and justice in intra-ecclesiastical relationships; to resolve conflicts that arise among the faithful; to seek the correction of wrongdoers; to keep and pass on peace and harmony in Christian and religious communities; to protect the sanctity of marriage and family life; to safeguard the public good of the Church in the dioceses as a necessary climate for living together in charity and for the salvation of souls; to attempt to reconcile litigants in order to avoid trials; to carry on an untiring search for truth as the basis and guarantee of all justice.

If he is to be able to carry out these tasks, the judge must act with total dedication, true professionalism, impartiality, flexibility, honesty, charity, and a pastoral feeling. These tasks require that he should be given broad powers in directing the proceedings, a true and effective independence and a stability of office only dependent on his efficacy in fulfilling his functions. Some of these conditions are so important that, should it be necessary, in order to obtain them and safeguard them, I would not hesitate to propose that the administration of justice throughout the whole Church should be autonomous under the ultimate guidance of the Apostolic Signatura which is already entrusted with the task of overseeing and organizing tribunals.

## BASIC DIMENSIONS OF THE JUDICIAL FUNCTION

Let us now look briefly at some of the functions of the diocesan judge in order to establish his importance in the structure of the judicial function and to set them in a wider horizon.

### The Judge as Mediator of Justice

This is perhaps the title that fits the judicial function best. The judge is the mediator of justice because he applies the law to life through his sentences, makes sure that facts are consummate with right and rightly determines what is just. In the words of Aristotle recorded by St Thomas[2] and often applied to ecclesiastic judges by the magisterium, the judge has to be a living embodiment of justice, since his mission, in the words of Pius XII, 'is to reflect the very justice of God whether he is trying to resolve controversies or to repress crimes'.[3] It would perhaps be more accurate and more expressive to call him *Vicarius Justitiae* instead of *Vicarius Judicialis,* since the first expression gives a better idea of his function of servant, defender and guarantor of justice rather than a simple servant of the law and legality. It should not be forgotten that the diocesan judge is a religious judge concerned with religious questions in a religious community and the justice he adminis-ters therefore possesses a theological and apostolic import: 'his whole action tends to show the Church, the Bride of Christ, holy and immaculate before her divine spouse and before men'.[4] This task of mediation requires honesty, objectivity, impartiality, independence, understanding, charity, and zeal for truth on the part of the judge.

If the diocesan judge is not to become a mediator of injustice, he has to offer the faithful a form of justice that is acceptable to all, effective and fair. His justice has to be quick since delay is already a form of injustice. This requires total dedication to his task and close attention through the whole proceedings: speed in admitting a plaint, firmness in rejecting worthless cases, incidents that can cause delay, irrelevant proof and unjustifiable delays. His justice also has to be economical since expensive justice, particularly in the Church, is an intolerable form of injustice. Still more there must be access to free justice through the diocesan tribunals, and if necessary a way of excluding lawyers who demand excessive fees, or a body of clerks formed who would serve the ecclesiastical tribunals with a fixed salary as their full-time service. The judge finally must sentence in conformity with the law, since this is a guarantee protecting those who are to be sentenced against injustices that the judge could commit through error, ignorance, haste, interest, prejudice or partiality.

As mediator of justice, the diocesan judge has to adopt a dynamic and creative attitude to the field of law and to be a creator of jurisprudence. In the secular field judicial power, the third of the political powers, was effectively broken by Montesquieu when he defined the judge as 'the mouth that pronounces the words of the law', thereby depriving him of any creative function in the field of law through jurisprudence. In the Church the jurisprudential creativity of the judge is practically non-existent since the Roman Rota is the only body allowed to take new initiatives in jurisprudence. The work of the diocesan judge is thereby impoverished with the consequence that cultural differences between the various peoples in which Catholicism exists are ignored. A way must be found for the diocesan judge to recover the noblest, most creative and human of his functions—that of jurisprudential initiative. The judge is not a simple instrument or minister of the power he holds, as Paul VI has said: he who holds the power of sanctification is only a minister or instrument of it, but he who holds the power of jurisdiction, as the judge does, is 'the responsible executor and secondary cause of it',[5] whose effective subordinate dynamism should be reflected in the work he carries out. In the same way, the judge should hold judicial control of ecclesiastical legislation which is a function not provided for in the Church and one that would be exercised in the case of the diocesan judge on the basic rules governing the diocese.

## The Judge as Protector of Individual Rights

The judge in the name of the bishop is the safeguarder of the individual rights of the faithful. This is why the judicial function exists. The judge must then recognise, declare, guarantee, uphold and re-instate the individual rights of the faithful. The judge guards the special good of the faithful in a direct and immediate way, unlike the legislator and governor whose task is to seek the common good directly and immediately. Therefore the judge cannot sacrifice the good of individuals to common good, since if he damages individual interests he also harms the common good, fails to co-operate in order, peace and the justice of the community which is the immediate object of the judicial function. This function of safeguarding individual rights is so important that in the new Codex the title *De processibus* will be replaced by *De modo procedendi pro tutela iurium*.

If he is to be able to function as mediator of justice and guardian of personal rights, the scope of the diocesan judge's activities must be widened. Where multi-diocesan tribunals are to be created, the diocesan judge should keep his competence alongside the regional tribunal in order to give the faithful easier access to justice, since they would have the right of choice in the same way as is provided for in cases that can go through the summary procedure. The promoter should be the competent judge in litigation between physical or moral persons belonging to the same religious institute of pontifical foundation, since the small volume of litigation would not justify the existence of judges among religious and would make it difficult to find suitable persons with sufficient professional training to act as judges.

The diocesan judge should have the ordinary power to instruct proceedings for non-consummation and dissolution in favour of the faith, without needing to have this power delegated by the Bishop, since although it is not a judicial function it is normally the judges who instruct in these proceedings. The same would have to be applicable to proceedings for reduction to the lay state.

Despite the choice that has already been made in the plan for reforming procedural law I would consider that administrative justice, or judicial control of its administration, should be in the hands of the ordinary metropolitan or regional tribunals instead of creating special administrative tribunals for this purpose as these are unnecessary in view of the indivisibility of power in the Church. Jurisdictional unity is also desirable in the Church and sufficient variety in proceedings can be achieved by creating administrative sections within the ordinary tribunals if this should prove necessary.

The diocesan judge could also act in a number of other ways not strictly judicial but nonetheless concerned with safeguarding and deciding any cases of individual rights, following the primitive apostolic tradition; the judge in the name of the bishop could be arbitrator and mediator even in temporal disputes among the faithful, even though his decision would have no effect with the secular arm.

## The Judge as Investigator of Truth

The ecclesiastical judge according to John XXIII exercises a *ministerium veritatis*.[6] Since a trial is merely an instrument for discovering objective and historical truth, and a sentence is an act that gives legal value to the truth, procedural practices should not be allowed to be manipulated so as to become an impediment to knowledge of the truth. Objective truth is the fruit of collaboration between all who take part in the trial and therefore it is essential that instruction in secret should be suppressed if those acting for the different parties are to help effectively in investigating the truth. Judge and counsel cannot go on being different worlds separated by misunderstandings and suspicions.

The judge must make every effort to avoid any discrepancy between procedural and historical truth, taking full account of his power to direct the proceedings, to instruct, and freely to evaluate truth. The importance of truth as the basis of justice makes it even more important that it is the same judge who instructs the case who passes sentence and that more trust and probatory value is placed on judicial confession and proof given in witness.

## The Judge as Minister of a Truly Pastoral Service

The administration of justice in the Church is a function of the care of souls since it derives from the pastoral power and care contained in the power of the keys. To see the judicial function in the Church as otherwise than at the service of salvation of souls would be to 'place it outside the end and unity of action proper to the Church as a divine institution'.[7] Paul VI has spoken equally vigorously on the subject: the judicial official is 'in the full sense of the word pastoral . . . he forms part of the apostolic mandate . . . this ministry is a pastoral one since it is designed to help members of the people of God who find themselves in difficulty. For them the judge is the good shepherd who consoles the wronged, guides the erring, recognises the rights of anyone who has been damaged, calumniated or unjustly humiliated. Judicial authority is therefore an authority of service, a service that consists in the exercise of the power entrusted by Christ for the good of the soul'.[8]

It is unfortunate that the clergy themselves often doubt or underestimate the important pastoral dimension of ecclesiastical tribunals. The judge receives part of the bishop's pastoral charge from the bishop and thereby becomes an authentic pastor to those seeking justice. Remember the words of Pius XII: 'the Holy Spirit calls bishops no less to the office of judges, than to government of the Church'.[9] All this requires that the judge should display an evangelical, charitable and merciful attitude, that he should maintain an open understanding and patience of mind, that he should be concerned to seek justice that both cures and educates at the same time. The pastoral ministry of the judge is a silent and hard one, but nonetheless sufficiently inspiring to encourage the best applicants. The wealth of his experience should make the diocesan judge the keystone of matrimonial and pre-matrimonial pastoral care in the diocese and an indispensable monitor to prevent matrimonial breakdowns and crises. His absence from diocesan councils and pastoral bodies, as is often the case, is inexplicable.

Finally I would like to warn against one possible misunderstanding that can arise from the pastoral nature of the diocesan judge's function: that of regarding it as a priestly or clerical function. Behind this conception lies the idea that the whole apostolate is a clerical task. I would say that today there are no valid reasons why this official should continue to be a priest whereas there are valid reasons why he could be a lay person.

CONCLUSION

It has been said that judicial jurisdiction is at the moment a sort of poor relation in the Church. The causes of the situation are well enough known not to need further analysis. I would like to say merely that the mission of the diocesan judge will never be treated with the importance it deserves until bishops come to realise what is virtually a judicial axiom: that justice is a matter of men rather than of laws; until consequently there is a more scientific system of training for judicial functions which would assure professional selection and capability in judges; until the judicial function is treated with more esteem and consequently requires greater ecclesiastical, pastoral and even economic dignity; and finally until judges are stimulated by being able to rise to tribunals with greater range and prestige.

*Translated by Paul Burns*

## Notes

1. Cf. J.-J. Toharia, *El juez español: un análisis sociológico* (Madrid, 1975), p. 102.

2. *ST* I–II, q. 60, a. lc.

3. Address to the Holy Roman Rota, 2 Oct. 1945, in *AAS* 37 (1945), p. 256.

4. *Ibid.,* p. 262.

5. Address to the Holy Roman Rota, 27 Jan. 1969, in *AAS* 61 (1969), p. 174.

6. John XXIII, Address . . . , 13 Dec. 1961, in *AAS* 53 (1961), p. 819.

7. Pius XII, Address . . . , 2 Oct. 1944, in *AAS* 36 (1944), p. 289.

8. Address . . . , 8 Feb. 1973, in *AAS* 65 (1973), p. 100.

9. Pius XII, Address . . . , 27 Oct. 1947, in *AAS* 39 (1947), p. 497.

Jean Bernhard

# Who Is to Judge?

BEFORE attempting to answer the question set, of who is to judge, one should first, it seems to me, ask oneself whether it is possible in today's Church to reply to this question at all in a satisfactory and convincing manner. Furthermore, is it still feasible that the judges of the Church—whatever they are called and whatever their collaborators are called—to fulfil the rôle that seems to be allocated to them in the heart of the Christian community? I am well aware of the difficulty of answering these questions, but it seems preferable to face them head on and to attempt an examination of the actual situation before proposing the deep renewal required by adaptation to the broad lines of the second Vatican Council and the pressing requirements of Christians today. It is only through this renewal that officialdom will be able to win back the confidence of pastors and lay people and present a truly evangelical and authentically pastoral image of itself. Reform, of course, can only be accomplished without damaging personal individual rights and equally without damaging doctrinal integrity.

My function here is not to situate the exact subject of this article in the whole theme of this number; my aim is more modest and more definite: my task is to foresee a widening of the function of judging, including lay people and experts within it . . . I would like, then, leaving the technical aspect of the problem to one side, to envisage the creation of official *teams,* in the full sense of the word, who would be charged with taking on a service or ministry of the 'defence of personal rights' of believers.

Three observations will set the scene and extent of the subject:

When I speak of *church* judges, I refer to the Church in western Europe in particular. The situation in the United States, for example, seems to be very different. Let us not exaggerate, however: there are certain *principles* of reform that can be usefully applied throughout the universal Church.

On all sides, voices can be heard demanding the setting-up of 'administrative tribunals' in the Church. This is undoubtedly an important result of the spirit of brotherhood and the synodal dimension introduced by Vatican II. These tribunals will naturally be structured differently from the 'matrimonial commissions' which already require a greater exercise of discretion. Because of the strict limits imposed on this article, I have had to choose, and I have decided to deal with matrimonial officialdom: this will allow me to base my remarks on long experience.

Despite the recent enlargement of the causes of nullity of marriage which allows them to be adapted to new developments in the human sciences and to include, for example, various forms of psychological immaturity, incapacity to fulfil (and to take on) the requirements of marriage . . . despite these definite signs of progress (provided these heads of nullity in the psychological domain are not made convenient but unreliable 'holdalls') the matrimonial commissions still cannot give a satisfactory answer to all the painful cases submitted to them. Rather than abandoning remarried divorcees to their fate if they have not been able to obtain a decree of nullity, the judges of the matrimonial commission should be forced to foresee an extension of responsibility capable of channelling the 'wild' pastoral practice which has been introduced more or less everywhere and which needs to be better founded theologically. I will deal further on with this problem and with that of the administrative tribunals.

For the sake of analysis, I will set out the principles that should guide and inspire the renovation of official bodies that I am proposing, before briefly setting out their essential characteristics; I hope thereby to bring out some main lines of direction and some new courses to be followed in the setting-up of a renewed official team. However, I would like to recall very briefly that in this field, we are facing a new set of problems. This is because the environment has changed within both civil society and the Church.

In all countries the number of divorces has increased considerably and attitudes to the divorced have changed; for the great majority of our contemporaries, the divorced person is no longer a 'deviant'. There is a marked tendency in the direction of procedures to facilitate divorce . . . Public opinion complains of the length of time the process takes, of the expense of the court procedures and of their formalism, and of judicial methods badly adapted to the present day world . . . Within the Church the same criticisms can be seen at work and they carry even more weight in view of the deep divergences between the number of divorces and the number of conjugal situations referred to the matrimonial commission. If the ministry of the matrimonial commissions is to become creative and active once more, it must respond to the aspirations of Christians and seek to change outlooks, though without falling into any excess. If this is to be done, the most important task is to inform pastors and lay people of the many services that officialdom can render at the present time by virtue of the deepening of theological understanding of marriage, of the contribution made by the human sciences, and of recent evolution in canon law.

One last preliminary remark: despite appearances, the need for justice in the Church has never been as great as it is at the present time. Let us not forget that if justice is to be truly just, it must seek inspiration from charity and fairness. Keeping these considerations in mind, I am now going to undertake three different approaches to the subject. There are three general tendencies that require attention and these are each plans that can help us along the route that has to be followed today.

## THE PASTORAL APPROACH

From strictly judicial considerations, we must now pass to the pastoral approach without abandoning canonical method and competence.

The creation of matrimonial tribunals in a response to a theological need: that of acquiring moral certitude on the inexistence or inconsistence of a sacramental bond so as to open the way to a new marriage. In the course of time, the legal and judicial aspects have come practically to eliminate the theological dimension. The moment has now come for church judges to adopt a more balanced way of acting, one better in accord with canon law. 'If the law of the Church is to have the value of being a sign of the inner action of the Spirit, it must express and favor the life of the Spirit, be an instrument of grace and a bond of unity but on a lower and different level from that of the sacraments . . . The first task (of the canonists) will therefore not be the establishment of a juridical order based purely on civil law, but to deepen the action of the Spirit which must also be expressed in the law of the Church'.[1]

'Thanks to canonical equity, the judge will take account of everything suggested by charity and everything allowed to avoid the full rigour of the law and rigidity of its technical expression . . .

'He would take account of the human person and of the needs of this situation which, if they sometimes impose on him the duty of applying the law more severely, would generally lead to an exercise of law that is more human and more understanding'.[2] In short, the matrimonial commissions which act in a field where they are dealing with human failings and infidelities above all, should also express divine mercy in their ministry.

The judicial matrimonial tribunal, whose proceedings were worked out in the twelfth century, was justified at this time, when the matrimonial conflicts submitted to the judgment of the Church concerned the nobility above all and brought serious consequences in the temporal order with them: it was then right for precise and rigid rules to be followed . . . In our days, when we put the stress on the interpersonal relationship of marriage, there are urgent indications that what is needed is a more visibly evangelical spirit in canonical matrimonial procedure. It is well known that Roman civil law, which is the basis of canonical judicial procedure, was a better instrument for serving the institution that the person.

Let it not be thought for a moment, however, that I am proposing a permissive solution: there can be no substitute for the guarantee and security conferred by canonical technique. It is not a question of substituting some so-called pastoral commission—in this context the term is very ambiguous—for the canonical commission; what is needed, on the contrary, is that the latter should act in a more evangelical spirit and with more evangelical methods, but there is no doubt that a truly deep renewal of the present system requires competent personnel to carry it out, hence the interest in establishing regional official teams (several dioceses regrouped to put their qualified personnel at the disposal of the whole group); the usefulness, indeed the need, to create centres for instruction in the various official functions as well as centres of further education; hence the need for local officials to maintain close links with faculties or institutes of canon law. Such links will be beneficial both to the teachers and to the practitioners of Canon Law; the first will be forced to tie their teaching to the actualities of life and the second will be obliged to base their judgments on better theological and canonical understanding. The lack of qualified and competent personnel has already led to the weakness of reform projects based on the postulate that there will always be a lack of qualified personnel, such as the extension of the single judge system. For the present and for the immediate future, one must accept the existence of situations that are regrettable in themselves, we have to admit, but the real failure would be to accept such a situation as permanent; it would be better to regroup judges and officials while planning at the same time for the instruction of new judges and new official teams.

This is perhaps the point at which I should mention the delicate problem of modifying judicial vocabulary, at least in so far as matrimonial procedures are concerned. Current terminology: ecclesiastical tribunal, judge, advocate, promoter of justice, defender of the bond . . . can hardly be considered adequate when what is at stake is the making of a religious 'judgment' in the heart of a religious community. I do not have space to go fully into this important question here, but I would just like to remark that the church 'judges' should from now on try to avoid intimidation or giving themselves the character of members of a civil court. They must also make sure that their correspondence with plaintiffs and witnesses moves away from juridical style and hermetic expressions . . .[3]

### THE CONSTITUTION OF A TEAM

The judicial tribunal in which each official operates on his own and from a particular angle (which is therefore partial and limited) must be replaced by the formation of a true team whose members are all called to resolve the same problem before taking on a particular function within the team.

Let there be no misunderstanding on the deep significance of this aspect of reform. It is absolutely not a simple matter of procedure, but of the whole way of undertaking the examination and study of cases submitted to the matrimonial commission that is in question. Contrary to what one sometimes reads, teamwork seems better adapted to the ministry of officialdom, particularly at a time when recourse to experts is becoming more and more necessary (particularly with grounds for nullity in the psychological domain). Furthermore, the ideal would be to reach a point when the plaintiffs and the witnesses can be made to understand that they too are intimately associated with the research team, if one can put it that way. Many difficulties would disappear if such a team spirit could be established. When the parties to the dispute can come to realize that the whole team is at their service, reform will be proceeding along the right lines.

An analysis of the procedure which leads up to the 'judgment' or final decision is sufficient to appreciate that teamwork is becoming more and more necessary. When one has to understand inner attitudes (such as the intention of excluding fidelity or indissolubility) the active participation of the interested parties themselves is particularly important. The reconstitution of external events will always be very imperfect. The judge has to assemble sparse facts and give them a meaning. Of course, he has to take his final decision alone, but this does not prevent the team from collecting specific proofs in common and trying to reach a more objective understanding of the situation together— since every judge has his psychological and theological horizons and these are more or less limited.

In order to illustrate my way of thinking, I would put forward the following suggestions:

More importance should be given to the declarations made by the interested parties. Of course, it should be explained to them that God is not mocked and that an apparently favourable decision, but one based on their lies, cannot be any use to them in conscience. The judges should therefore receive the applicants with goodwill, confidence and respect. Throughout the investigation they must remember that they have to be careful not to violate individual rights.

In order to integrate counsel for prosecution and defence better into the official team, I consider that the different stages of the enquiry would gain from being prepared by all members of the team together with none being reduced to the role of simple executor.

Without insisting on the procedural aspect, I would like to stress at this point the importance of meetings of the whole team, first at the outset of the enquiry, and second towards the end of the "instruction" stage.

When someone wishes to submit his matrimonial situation to the matrimonial commission, he should be given, at the reception office, all useful information on the composition of the team charged with examining his situation as well as on the procedure that will be followed. It should be explained to him that his help will be very necessary if everything is to go ahead as quickly as possible. During this preliminary interview, the petitioner would have a chance to set out his situation freely and spontaneously, concentrating particularly on the events leading up to his marriage, the course of his married life and what led to the break. The notes taken by the person conducting the interview, assisted by the petitioner himself, would be immediately sent to the advocate and the defender of the bond. The interview between the petitioner and his advocate would complete and clarify the first interview, putting important events and behaviour patterns into context, and the ways of proving them, so leading to the drawing-up of a request for a declaration of nullity. The first meeting of the commission would follow, during which the nullity grounds would be decided and more technical interviews prepared: the questionnaires drawn up in this way would allow the elements of the case to be set out more precisely and more specifically. These exchanges would be far shorter than in the past. The first meeting of the team would also serve to eliminate the less important witnesses.

The second session of the commission would deal with the outcome of the previous exchanges. The team would then be joined by the two assessing judges. The members of the commission, laying aside their specific roles of judge, advocate, and so on, would examine the situation 'objectively', noting the points susceptible to different interpretations. At the same time the supplements detailing further research, if necessary, would be prepared. Of course, the views stemming from this meeting would not tie the members of the team in any way, whether they are judge, defender of the bond, or advocate.

Team spirit could also play a useful part at the final meeting of the three judges (each one accepting, for example, to pursue a particular point in greater depth without, of course, losing sight of the overall aspects of the case) and even in their relationships with the appeal tribunal. If a declaration of nullity is given, appeal would not be obligatory unless it was demanded by the defender of the bond and one of the judges in the first case. Perhaps the judges and the team responsible for the second hearing could simply be asked to enquire deeper into particular points that had caused difficulties at the first hearing?

## LAY AND EXPERT PARTICIPANTS

The official team should be open to lay people and to experts; it should act in closer liaison with local communities and perhaps—particularly when it is dealing with cases involving what I have referred to above as 'extension of the responsibility of officialdom'—with organizations dealing in family care. It would in any case be desirable for persons involved in such a pastoral ministry to become part of the official team after they had received the requisite instruction: such collaboration would benefit both them and the team.

One word only on the importance of experts in the official sphere. The enhanced rôle of psychologists and psychiatrists stems above all from the introduction of new grounds for nullity, of a psychological kind. These could be, for example, inability to carry out (or to take on) the duties of marriage, or psychological immaturity, implying a deficiency of the estimative and critical faculties and anything that seriously hampers freedom of choice.

Pursuing this aspect of the problem would take me away from my subject: it will have to suffice to note that these grounds for nullity take different forms in practice and that refusing expert help in these matters would seriously risk compromising right judgment and damaging the personal rights of the petitioners. In this field, it would be equally useful for psychologists to acquire a basic canonical formation; this would undoubtedly make collaboration easier on both sides.

Another aspect of the opening-up of the official team is that of the active presence of lay people as part of the team itself. It should hardly be necessary to say again that it is not a question merely of appealing to lay people because of a shortage of clerics or of the need to accelerate the proceedings. There are clear theological reasons why lay people should be involved in the responsibilities inherent in the mission of the Church; there are also clear human reasons why lay people should take part in the official workings of the Church, particularly in the matrimonial sphere. The proposed revision of the future code of canon law clearly states the principle of opening official tasks to lay people, but when it comes to particular applications there is an unjustifiable discrimination between men and women. The job of notary is the only one for which a woman is considered fit; a lay man can act as assessing judge or as 'examining magistrate', but for such a lay man to act as judge in a collegiate tribunal, he needs the authorisation of the episcopal Conference. It is also noticeable that the quota of lay men (one judge out of three) in a collegial tribunal corresponds to the practice of the Roman Curia in dealing with synodal forms of government: lay people cannot be in an absolute majority.

This approach, while it shows a certain distrust of lay people, does resolve the theological problem of lay participation in ecclesiastical authority in a purely empirical fashion. The difficulty has been seen, since a lay person can only form part of a collegial tribunal and is not qualified to fulfil the function of sole judge. One might ask how the second Vatican Council would have dealt with this question, since it declared that ecclesial power stemmed in its entirety from sacramental ordination. One thing is certain: the Council did not give any judicial power to deacons. In attempting to resolve this problem, some canonists consider the function of judge not to be one truly belonging to ecclesiastical authority (which is somewhat strange, to say the least!); others invoke the concept of delegated judiciary power, but exactly what is meant by the juridical nature of delegation under the rule of *potestas sacra* (Vatican II) stemming solely from sacramental ordination has yet to be clarified.

If we allow all pastoral authority to stem only from ordination, we either have to foresee sacramental ordination for all ministers of the Church (including lay people working in an official capacity), or we have to reserve ordination for the pastoral ministry in the strict sense of the term while admitting that pastoral authority in the wider sense can stem from baptism or perhaps confirmation. Personally, I would put forward this explanation: the deep intuition of Vatican II has been to emphasize the unity of ecclesial authority and to point out its sacramental origin: i.e., ordination for the exercise of apostolic authority in the strict sense, and baptism or confirmation for the exercise of pastoral care. This of course leaves the task of relating ordination more specifically to baptism in this field still to be done. In any case, on the level of the official team, the theological principle will be safeguarded if one reserves the roles of president of the collegial tribunal and perhaps of defender of the bond to ordained ministers.

Officials must act in close liaison with local communities, that is, with parishes and parish priests. This collaboration can take place on different levels. On one hand, because of the present evolution of canonical doctrine and jurisprudence, the official team must organize an information service for itself: this could take the form of sessions or meetings with parish priests, or parish priests and lay people together, dealing with the present-day pastoral ministry of officialdom; or canonical consultations addressed to those whose marriage has ended in failure. On the other hand, the local communities should participate more fully in the official ministry. Why not, for example, form a team in each deanery that would be responsible for the pastoral care of 'irregularly' remarried divorced people? When dealing with cases that have been referred to the diocesan matrimonial commission, these deanery teams could play various parts such as issuing certificates of 'honourableness' duly witnessed (it would no longer be a question simply of signing a formula prepared in advance), giving their views at the outset of the proceedings on the matrimonial situation itself: what the reasons for the break were; whether the future partner played a part in disrupting the marriage; the situation of the first partner, children born of the first marriage, and so on.

If the present rate of increase in marital breakdown continues, it is foreseeable that—if information is given prudently but effectively—the number of matrimonial cases submitted to the commission will go on growing. To a greater extent, certain interviews with witnesses will have to be carried out at the witnesses' homes. It will therefore become essential to give at least some form of canonical instruction to a certain number of members of deanery commissions such as those I have been talking about.

CONCLUSION

I am very conscious of the gaps in this article, which deals only with a limited part of diocesan official proceedings in matrimonial matters: that is, the area of declarations of nullity. There are many places where I would have liked to amplify and illustrate, but I would then have missed the objective set for this article, which was to give an overall view in which the essential lines of the problem could be at least set out.

The choice I have made in sticking to declarations of nullity should not invalidate the basic situation: faced with irremediable breakdown of marriage, the official ministry can no longer today be content with the traditional system of declaration of nullity, whatever its pastoral interests and its theological and canonical justifications may be. Everyone is becoming increasingly aware that a new approach is needed: here, one can do no more than pose the problem, which I see as one of the most urgent of those facing the Church today.

*Translated by Paul Burns*

### Notes

1. Paul VI, 'Allocution to the International Congress of Canon Law' (17 Sep. 1973), in *La documentation catholique* 70 (1973), p. 804.
2. Paul VI, 'Equity in Canon Law' (8 Feb. 1973), in *La documentation catholique* 70 (1973), p. 206.
3. For the sake of clarity, I use the traditional judicial vocabulary, for which I beg the reader's pardon.

Thomas Green

# A Living Jurisprudence

ANY living legal system is in a state of constant development. Since Vatican II there has been a noteworthy evolution of various canonical institutes. This is especially evident in ecclesiastical marriage jurisprudence.[1] Yet profound questions are being raised about the credibility of Church courts.[2] The stresses of contemporary Church renewal are perhaps no more evident than in the marital nullity process—a sophisticated effort to preserve the basic Gospel values of marital indissolubility and divine reconciliation for sinners.[3]

The formal judicial process of Book IV of the Code of Canon Law envisions more than marriage cases. Yet *de facto,* at least in the United States, this is usually the exclusive business of church courts. Modern pressures on married life have occasioned an extremely high divorce rate and increasing access to church courts for a clarification of ecclesial status. This has promoted intensified scrutiny of the tribunal system and evaluation of the vitality of its jurisprudence.

Jurisprudence here means the art of applying, interpreting and supplying for the codified law by judicial sentence. It is a pattern of uniform decisions in marriage cases. It is also the authority of such decisions because of their legal wisdom or the calibre of the court, e.g. the Roman Rota.[4]

The vitality of jurisprudence depends on the persons deciding marriage cases, the decisional process and the criteria for determining marital nullity. Each of these interrelated elements will be examined to clarify those factors crucial to a living jurisprudence, i.e., a jurisprudence reflecting the basic values of our theologico-legal tradition.

### THE DECISION MAKERS

Two key issues here are the relationship between the Roman Rota and other courts and the composition of the court in marriage cases.

Despite periods of decline, the Rota has traditionally been the most significant church court in marriage nullity cases. Other courts, however significant, often have waited for Rotal authorization of newer jurisprudential paths and have failed to exercise a genuinely creative rôle. Furthermore there has been little professional dialogue between the Rota and other courts.

Another problem has been the practice of officially publishing Rota decisions only after ten years. Certain decisions appear in canonical journals before official publication; yet this somewhat sporadic, haphazard approach is hardly conducive to systematic jurisprudential development.

The great conciliar document on the nature of the Church, *Lumen gentium,* paragraph 23, has emphasized that fundamental unity in faith, worship and governance does not exclude but rather is to be harmonized with legitimate theological, liturgical and ascetical diversity. Such diversity seems appropriate regarding the interrelationship of Church courts. There should be greater freedom of initiative for non-Roman courts to develop a jurisprudence faithfully reflecting the customs, usages and aspirations of the people they serve.[5] Slavish uncritical dependence on Rotal decisions hardly enhances jurisprudence or clarifies the theological-legal reality of marriage. This is especially true when there is no real consensus among Rotal judges themselves on a given point.

Interestingly enough during the past decade there has been increased creativity by non-Roman courts. The recent publication of significant decisions by American, British and Canadian courts among others reflects their increased importance in shaping a more vital jurisprudence.[6]

While jurisprudential diversity is a value, there also is a value in greater contact between court personnel in various countries. Obviously the above-mentioned publication of decisions will facilitate awareness of different court practices. The Rota (or perhaps the Apostolic Signatura) might facilitate a personal exchange of views and experiences by various court personnel. However, this should not be an effort to foster an artificial uniformity but rather to stimulate and protect legitimate differences not threatening Church unity.

Another key issue is the composition of Church courts. Generally judges in marriage cases have been clerics. The laity may be advocates and notaries yet not judges except occasionally and only if they are laymen. Certainly the fact that clerics are male and celibate does not preclude their judging wisely in marriage cases. However, the value of the lived experience of married couples and the growing awareness of the integral ecclesial rôle of the laity raise questions about the continuing vitality of a system not taking adequate cognizance of married persons' input in the decisional process. Furthermore, at a time of serious re-examination of the ecclesial rôle of women, their exclusion from an integral part in judging marriage cases is increasingly perplexing.

There is a noticeable shift taking place in nullity cases from a strongly juridical decisional process to one stressing marriage as a personal relationship and a spiritual sacramental reality. The courts are increasingly more concerned about the ambiguous realities of psychological motivation, commitment and capacity than about external behavior as in the past. The insights of experts in the human sciences are taken more seriously. However, perhaps the courts have underestimated the contribution of married couples in discerning signs of life or their absence in a marriage.[7]

Can a pre-eminently clerical nullity process realistically meet the pastoral needs of married couples or elicit their wholehearted cooperation? A continuing problem for the church courts is the lack of trained personnel especially given mounting caseloads. Accordingly this seems to be an area where the faith experience of trained married couples could be especially valuable. Who could better refine the courts' ability to perceive the relational skills of couples and their ability to grow into a community of life and love? Who could offer more perceptive insights into a couple's ability to symbolize the Lord's self-giving to his Church? There is seemingly no better way of incorporating such wisdom into the decisional process and facilitating dialogue between canonists and the community than by making mixed lay-clerical pastoral teams a systematic part of the jurisprudential process.[8] Decisions made by such teams would more likely be credible to married couples since they would probably be more firmly rooted in the life of the community.[9]

Fidelity to its calling means the Church is to respond to the three-fold challenge of society, other churches and its own anti-discrimination tradition by providing for serious involvement of women in the decisional process in marriage cases. It is not only reasonable but just that women should take part in the adjudication of marriage cases. The issue is not ordination. The issue is not jurisdiction, since laymen are judging certain cases. The issue is rather the possibility for women to express their personhood fully not only in the light of sexual determinants but primarily in view of God-given qualities of freedom, intellect and affectivity. These qualities have been amply demonstrated in the secular legal arena. An ecclesial process failing to enhance their exercise cannot long maintain its credibility.[10]

## THE PROCESS

Admittedly there have been significant post-conciliar attempts at simplifying and expediting marriage cases, e.g. American Procedural Norms (1970)[11] and to a lesser extent the motu proprio *Causas Matrimoniales* (1971).[12] However, concern for a living jurisprudence responding to legitimate aspirations for a healing, liberating judgment in faith raises further questions about the viability of the present nullity process. In personal crisis situations individuals are more likely to be guided by therapeutic pastoral care than by a formal court judgment however procedurally correct. This is not pure subjectivism but rather a deeper objectivity in which personal relationships are taken more seriously.[13] What is at stake is not simply a reform of certain procedural formalities but a reshaping of the basic orientation of the nullity process. It must be perceived unequivocally as pastoral, salvific, evangelical and distinctively ecclesial.[14]

For one thing, the present process is too strongly based on a conflict of rights situation. This is understandable given the history of the tribunal system and the political-economic implications of nullity decisions in various milieus. An adversary model, however, seems inappropriate in the sacramental arena where the basic issue is discerning the presence or absence of marital consent and/or capacity. This adversary approach is certainly out of place in most English-speaking countries where tribunal decisions have no civil law ramifications. Generally petitioners in marriage cases in these areas are primarily if not exclusively concerned about peace of conscience and full participation in the sacramental life of the Church. Yet, unfortunately, the rather ponderous court apparatus has often alienated from the institutional Church those individuals most in need of its service in clarifying their ecclesial status.

A fundamental way of dealing with the above issues is by transforming the ecclesiastical process into a search for truth about marital commitment pursued in a less rigidly juridical fashion. Instead of a tribunal hardly differing from secular analogates, what is called for is a pastoral team scrutinizing marital validity from a theologico-legal standpoint yet scrupulously respecting the rights of all involved in the process. Rather than settling a conflict of rights, such a pastoral team would collaborate in bringing diverse insights to bear upon marital breakdown so as to discern the quality of and/or the capacity for a genuine marital commitment. Possible models for such a search for truth process are present canonization and laicization procedures, which are less rigidly juridical, simpler, founded primarily on pastoral criteria yet are oriented to the perception of objective truth.[15]

Another key procedural problem related to the conflict of rights focus has been the development of an elaborate set of procedural norms more reflective of civil law techniques than of an evangelical process of discernment, inspired more by Roman law models than by the Gospel. Frequently the decisional process has exalted institutional values over personal spiritual concerns. The profoundly educative and reconciliatory character of a distinctively ecclesial process has frequently been overshadowed by excessive concern for juridical precision and formalities.

A properly ecclesial system, on the contrary, must stress the primacy of pastoral service as its dominant motif. If those experiencing marital breakdown are to be aided by the system, the decision regarding marital validity must be a primarily religious one situated within the broader context of ministry to the divorced. A sincere desire to rebuild their lives in Christ prompts most petitioners to approach the court. Procedural formalities must respect the integrity of such individuals and hence need not be as elaborately structured as in the past when at times collusion and deceit were not uncommon in church courts. A truly vital jurisprudence is inseparable from a process administering justice in a way that is efficient, rapid, equitable and accessible to all. This accessibility presupposes that the community at large and especially ministerial leaders are aware of the latest developments in jurisprudence. Above and beyond the publication of decisions in professional journals, continuing efforts should be made to inform the wider community of their legal-pastoral options. This must be done, however, in such a way as to protect the legitimate rights of confidentiality of those involved in marriage cases.

## CRITERIA OF DECISION

At times nullity decisions may appear somewhat artificial since they seem minimally related to the existential factors influencing marital breakdown. However, this may be more true about a process declaring marriage null because the parties did not solemnize their consent in the prescribed form than of a process exploring a lack of marital capacity or a deficient marital commitment: e.g., intentions contrary to basic Christian values such as children, permanence and fidelity.

A credible nullity process must be related to factors affecting the human and Christian values of marriage. Otherwise individuals may be satisfied with an annulment since they may enter into or validate a second marriage. Yet the process will have little impact on them as an education in faith and a preparation for a genuinely Christian second union. This education presupposes not only a clarification of the nullity of the first marriage but also an effort at specifying the human and Christian obligations flowing from that marriage.

At the heart of a truly living jurisprudence are the criteria of ecclesial decision regarding marital validity.

In reflecting on the Church's jurisprudence, John Noonan sees certain key elements at work as the Church strives to accommodate various values fundamental to the system: social custom, particularly European, inherited theology, Scripture, Roman law and community beliefs.

The synthesis of various criteria for decision is basic to the jurisprudential process. The creativity and integrity of this synthesis largely determine the living quality of jurisprudence. The heart of any dynamic legal system is the formulation of basic values and their application in particular circumstances. Jurisprudence will cease being vital and will be minimally credible to the extent that certain values are overemphasized and others given minimal if any attention. Likewise a vital jurisprudence is retarded by rigidly clinging to one formulation of a value (e.g., indissolubility) even when such a formulation should be modified because of new insights.

What are some components of a vital contemporary jurisprudence? First and foremost, jurisprudence must be grounded on a solid biblico-theological understanding of Christian marriage. Today jurisprudence can profit greatly from the magisterial teaching of *Casti connubii*, *Gaudium et spes* and *Humanae vitae* as well as from theologico-canonical reflection on their insights. There is a significantly new emphasis on marriage as a covenant rather than a contract, on the indispensable value of conjugal love as more than a secondary end of marriage and on a total giving of self as essential to a marital communion of life. This notably changes the Code's specification of the object of marital consent as the permanent and exclusive right to the spouse's body for procreative acts (canon 1081, 2). *Gaudium et spes* especially focuses attention on marriage as a total life partnership. It transcends a formerly heavy emphasis on institutional/procreative values and accords proper weight to the marriage vocation, the mutual perfection of the spouses.

Undeniably, recent years have seen increased use of psychological insights in the nullity process. However, still more fundamental to our understanding of Christian marriage are distinctively theological insights. Perhaps in the past the theology of marriage was relatively undeveloped and was overly influenced by distinctively juridical concerns. We take for granted that theology is not law nor law theology. However, unless law is shaped by theological insights, it will be a sterile enterprise and unworthy of a faith community. Happily theology once again seems to be reasserting its rightful priority over canon law in marriage jurisprudence. Marriage has an undeniably juridical character, which is not to be underestimated. Yet our understanding of marriage must always be deduced from and oriented to theology.[16]

In this connection the faithful living of Christian marriage has not played its proper rôle in the elaboration of a theology of marriage. Such theology must be rooted in biblical, traditional, and magisterial data. But it must also have deep roots within the existential experience of couples struggling to embody in their lives the Lord's covenant with his people. As the nullity process focuses more sharply on the dynamics of the marital relationship it will have to be informed more and more by the wisdom of the lived experience of couples. Increased lay theological literacy enhances the possibility of spouses' articulating the meaning of their life together. The Church must facilitate the incorporation of such insights into the theological and jurisprudential process.

In the present ecumenical period, official/unofficial conversations foster more perceptive awareness of other religious traditions. Furthermore, pastoral concern for the quality of married life and ministry to the divorced are by no means an exclusively Roman Catholic concern. Accordingly, the absence of serious dialogue with other churches in this area deprives us of access to the wisdom of these traditions. Despite theological differences, that wisdom might well aid us greatly in grappling with the various interrelated issues involved in marital breakdown. Theologico-biblical-historical research and pastoral practice have been enhanced by contact with scholars and pastors of other traditions. Jurisprudence would well be likewise enriched. This is particularly true as we move away from somewhat legalistic standards of past jurisprudence to a more pastoral emphasis on reconciliation, forgiveness and the healing of persons and families.[17]

A second notable factor in a living jurisprudence is the contribution of the human sciences, especially psychology. Especially since Pius XII in 1941 encouraged increased recourse to the human sciences, the courts have refined their understanding of psychic factors affecting marital capacity. Particularly since the beginning of the nineteensixties, there have been significant developments in so-called 'lack of due discretion' cases.[18]

Capacity for the demanding interpersonal relationship that is marriage is normally presumed. However, experts in the human sciences have increasingly drawn attention to psychic disorders precluding either proper evaluation of what marriage involves or the fulfillment of essential marital obligations. Vatican II has stressed that couples must be capable of living out the interpersonal and procreative responsibilities of marriage if there is to be a true communion of life and love. This thrust has further reinforced the urgency of ongoing dialogue between the courts and experts in the human sciences. This exchange has not been without its problems, particularly as regards professional differences in concepts and terminology and in the interrelationships in particular cases of experts in the two fields. Yet it has stimulated the most significant contemporary jurisprudential development. Its impact is evident in the proposed new canons on marriage. For the first time different types of marital incapacity are explicitly mentioned: those deprived entirely of the use of reason because of a mental illness or serious disturbance of mind, those suffering from a serious defect of judgmental discretion regarding marital rights and obligations and those unable to undertake essential marital obligations because of a serious psychosexual disorder.[19]

Church law has traditionally stressed the ancillary rôle of the expert in assisting the judge to form moral certitude regarding the validity of a marriage. However, this rôle is often indispensable if the judge is perceptively to read the dynamics of the marital relationship. As the percentage of psychic incapacity cases rises, the need for continuing judge-expert contact increases. In fact the more that the jurisprudential process shifts from a heavily contractual to a more interpersonal model, the harder it becomes to distinguish sharply the respective rôles of the judge and the medical experts.[20]

Legal capacity for marriage is not necessarily the same as psychic capacity for marriage. Yet the theologically based emphasis on the importance of relational (covenantal) capacity notably shifts the ground on which legal decisions are based.

Experts in marriage cases traditionally have been psychologists, psychiatrists or psychiatric social workers offering insights into the capacity of parties for an interpersonal relationship. Yet an increasingly vital rôle will be played in future jurisprudence by experts in the other human sciences, notably sociology and cultural anthropology. This seems to be a third vital current influencing the criteria for marriage nullity decisions.

In a significant 1969 Rotal decision Anné suggested that a living marriage jurisprudence must take into consideration three key elements: the law of nature or marriage as a divinely intended institution and vocation understood in faith, the personalities of the spouses, and the environmental, familial and sociological circumstances of their culture.[21]

The above-mentioned experts should assist the court in perceptively reading cultural factors that are particularly significant as regards marital attitudes and values.

Among the sociological factors to be taken seriously in western society are the following: the movement towards occupational and socio-legal equality among the sexes, a more permissive attitude towards sexuality, an increasingly contraceptive focus among married couples, the less central place of the home in today's world, increased civil divorce options, increasing social acceptance of divorce as legitimate when marriage becomes intolerable, and so on.[22]

A jurisprudence failing to take cognizance of such elements in assessing understanding of and commitment to the traditional Christian marital values of permanence, children and fidelity would become increasingly irrelevant. It would be rash to assert that couples entering marriage are always predominantly influenced by and cannot challenge the values of their culture, especially those opposed to the Christian tradition. However it would be naive to suppose that they are not significantly affected by such values.

Respect for the legitimate diversity of Christian experience likewise suggests the inadequacy of a jurisprudence operating from postulates proper to only one culture however significant and practically prescinding from the pluriformity of the institution of marriage.

Noonan indicates that European sociocultural mores have been particularly significant in shaping Church jurisprudence. The stress on marriage as an interpersonal relationship is heavily dependent on the cultural values of western society.

Undoubtedly these values have significantly influenced Third World countries. However, socio-cultural research shows that numerous forms of marriage in different countries and cultures cannot be reconciled with the Roman notion of an irrevocable contract made at a particular moment and with absolute formality. African marriages, for instance, occur as a process over a long time, often several years. There may be societies in which such values as conjugal love and monogamy are not prevalent because of different experience and mythology. This is particularly true where the idea of marriage is almost interchangeable with the idea of the extended family and where a strong sense of community is all-pervading. Perhaps we in the West have not fully realized that in mankind as a whole there must be different, complementary and reciprocally stimulating expressions of married life. A truly vital jurisprudence must avoid the cultural and religious imperialism implicit in identifying Christian marriage with the interpersonal aspirations of the Western world.

William Schumacher perceptively indicates a two-fold approach to the development of a vital jurisprudence in this new and challenging area.[23]

First, anthropological, historical and sociological sciences must illumine the varying contexts in which marriage is lived. Second, theologians and historians must further clarify the Church's tradition on marriage, rooted as it is in divine revelation but incarnated in varying cultures. A vital jurisprudence must avoid two equally destructive tendencies: uncritically accepting every cultural manifestation of marriage even if dehumanizing and unevangelical, or casually rejecting every marital form outside our contemporary western experience.

### CONCLUSION

A living jurisprudence reflecting our theologico-legal tradition is a multi-faceted reality. It depends on various factors which have been briefly examined: a more significant rôle for non-Roman courts and a broadening of the decision-makers in marriage cases to include married couples, a de-juridicized process emphasizing the search for truth rather than the resolution of a conflict of rights and a continuing effort to integrate theological data and insights from all the human sciences.

The above ideas have been articulated elsewhere by different authors. Hopefully their being synthesized here will stimulate further reflection by canonists, specialists in other disciplines and the faithful at large especially married couples. Only the prayerful, informed collaboration of all within the community will facilitate refashioning ecclesial structures in view of a more effective mission.

*Notes*

1. Cf. Canon Law Society of Great Britain and Ireland, *The Church's Matrimonial Jurisprudence: A Statement on the Current Position* (Canon Law Society Trust, 1975).

2. Cf. L. Wrenn (ed.), *Divorce and Remarriage in the Catholic Church* (New York, 1973).

3. For a detailed historical analysis of the Church's nullity/dissolution practice cf. J. Noonan, *Power to Dissolve: Lawyers in the Courts of the Roman Curia* (Cambridge, Mass., 1972).

4. Cf. Z. Varalta, 'De iurisprudentiae conceptu,' *Periodica* 62 (1973) pp. 39–57. L. Wrenn, *Annulments,* 2nd ed. (Hartford, 1972), pp. 1–5, esp. 1–2.

5. The Code Commission committee on procedural law reform ostensibly seeks to balance the values of a certain necessary uniformity and a healthy

decentralization though it emphasizes the former. Cf. *Communicationes* 2 (1970), pp. 183 and 185 (points 7 and 13).

6. For selected United States decisions cf. A. Maida (ed.) *The Tribunal Reporter* (Huntington, Ind., 1970). Four succeeding volumes cover 1968–1974. For some Canadian decisions cf. Le Tribunal d'Appel Matrimonial, *Sentences* (Montreal, 1965–   ). For some British and Irish decisions see *Matrimonial Decisions for England and Wales* (Canon Law Society of Great Britain, 1967–   ).

7. E. Kennedy, 'Signs of Life in Marriage', in Wrenn, *Divorce and Remarriage,* pp. 121–133.

8. Cf. J. Finnegan, 'The Capacity to Marry', *The Jurist* 29 (1969), pp. 141–56 especially 153–6. Also P. Huizing, 'Alternativentwurf für eine Revision des Kanonischen Eherechts', in *Für eine neue Kirchliche Eheordnung,* ed. P. Huizing (Düsseldorf, 1975), pp. 97–102.

9. For a discussion of broader participation in the revision of marriage law see Report of a Special Committee of the Task Force of the Canon Law Society of America on the Marriage Canons of the Proposed *Schema Documenti Pontificii quo Disciplina Canonica de Sacramentis Recognoscitur,* in *Proceedings of the Thirty-Seventh Annual Convention of the Canon Law Society of America* (1975) pp. 213–6 (henceforth *Proceedings*).

10. Cf. Committee on the Status of Women in the Church, in *Proceedings,* 185–92. Also 'La mujer y la función judicial', *Ius Canonicum* 12 (1972), pp. 189–238.

11. Cf. *The Jurist* 30 (1970), pp. 363–8. See T. Green, 'The American Procedural Norms—an Assessment', *Studia Canonica* 8 (1974), pp. 317–47.

12. Cf. *Acta Apostolica Sedis* 63 (1971), pp. 441–6.

13. Huizing, *loc. cit.*

14. For a detailed analysis of the following issues cf. G. Lesage, 'Pour une rénovation de la procédure matrimoniale', *Studia Canonica* 7 (1973), pp. 253–79.

15. For canonization procedures cf. Paul VI, *motu proprio Sanctitas clarior, Acta Apostolica Sedis* 61 (1969), pp. 149–53. For laicization procedures cf. Circular letter of Sacred Congregation for the Doctrine of the Faith *Litteris encyclicis, Acta Apostolica Sedis* 63 (1971), pp. 203–312.

16. Cf. R. Sanson, 'Jurisprudence for Marriage: Based on Doctrine', *Studia Canonica* 10 (1976), pp. 5–36.

17. J. Wynne, 'Prevailing and Countervailing Trends in the Non-Catholic Churches', in Wrenn (ed.), *Divorce and Remarriage,* pp. 65–88.

18. Cf. W. LaDue, 'The Expanding Limits of Due Discretion Cases', *Concilium,* vol. 87, pp. 61–71.

19. Pontificia Commissio Codici Iuris Canonici Recognoscendo, *Schema Documenti Pontificii quo Disciplina Canonica de Sacramentis Recognoscitur* (Typis Polyglottis Vaticanis, 1975), Canons 296–297. Cf. *supra* note 9 for Canon Law Society Task Force Report. Also F. Morrisey, "The Incapacity of Entering into Marriage", *Studia Canonica* 8 (1974), pp. 5–21.

20. On the judge-expert interaction cf. J. Keating, 'The Province of Law and the Province of Forensic Psychiatry in Marriage Nullity Trials', *Studia*

*Canonica* 4 (1970), pp. 5–23. C. Lefebvre, 'De peritorum iudicumque habitudine in causis matrimonialibus ex capite amentiae', *Periodica* 65 (1976), pp. 107–22.

21. Cf. Rotal decision of February 25, 1969 *coram* Anné in *Ephemerides Iuris Canonici* 26 (1970), pp. 419–42.

22. Cf. J. Aubert, 'Declaration de nullité et société moderne,' *Revue de Droit Canonique* 26 (1976), pp. 67–78. (This volume of the *Revue de Droit Canonique* is especially valuable for its examination of the nullity process). B. Griffin, 'Future Challenges in the Area of Marriage Legislation', *Proceedings of the Thirty-Fifth Annual Convention of the Canon Law Society of America* (1973), pp. 22–32.

23. W. Schumacher, 'The Importance of Interpersonal Relations in Marriage', *Studia Canonica* 10 (1976), pp. 75–112.

William Bassett

# To Judge on the Merits of the Case

IN his letter to the professors and students of the University of
Bologna, *Rex Pacificus,* Pope Gregory IX explained that the purpose of
his new collection of decretals was to assist judges in making decisions
certain and well-informed.[1] A rule of law, he said quoting Ulpian,
should promote peace, help people live honorably, prevent injuries and
secure the rights of all. This letter began the first great papal initiative
to reform the canon law. The year was 1234. The letter was accom-
panied by a compilation made by Raymond of Peñafort of thousands of
papal decisions resolving doubts, settling disputes, healing injuries and
mediating mercy in the lives of persons all over the Christian world.

The decretals were paradigmatic of a rôle in the Church of persons
helping other persons by a primary concern for the facts and circumstances, the values and insights arising from the particular situations in
life. Their message was a ministry of reassurance, of peace and justice.
It was the written record of the experiences of wise and learned judges
shared with persons who would be called upon to make decisions in
similar matters in councils and synods, in chanceries and parish as-
semblies, on visitations, in chapter meetings and in the courts Christian, the tribunals. The decretals were law forged on practical experience; they were judge-made law, canons of decision arising out of the
confluence of life and faith. No person can tell another what his judgment should be in a particular case. The decretals are strikingly non-
apodictic. They are examples of how to judge, a mode of arriving at
decisions reflecting faith and charity. In a vital and creative era of the
Church's life, the decretal law supplied exemplary reference points of a
practical wisdom. Christian judges garnered and interpreted this practical wisdom further in decrees and opinions of their own, in mediation

and compromising disputes, in consultation and advice, literally to re-shape civilization, creating a Christian culture and leaving a permanent legacy of human values to permeate the western legal tradition.

I should like to use the decretal law to reflect upon several aspects of the ministry of judges in the churches. I take this starting point not out of nostalgia or even in an attempt to resurrect a lost and imperfect era. It is my thought, rather, to explain the tradition of the Church's law before it came to be codified and the authority of practical judgment relegated solely to the Roman dicasteries and tribunals. This tradition, I believe, reveals a ministry of judging in the churches that is dialectic and mediational. It is a ministry that of its very nature is creative, nonsacramental, relatively independent and uniquely nondidactic. It is a ministry of men and women who must, in the final analysis, express their own opinions in concrete circumstances, one case at a time, de-ciding what is right between persons, unbiased by institutional ideol-ogy. The charism of the judge in the classic canons is not to apply a preconceived law to every circumstance. It is, rather, to see the uniqueness in each and every person and to use the law as a single factor in a total perspective upon life's complexities to fashion in each case a new law. Judges make law; they do not merely apply laws. Reform of the ministry of judges means setting this precious charism free again.

## EACH CASE ON ITS OWN MERITS

Pope Innocent III, a great canon lawyer, once said, in answer to an inquiry from the bishop of Troyes, that a wise decision in ecclesiastical matters will be marked by three considerations: *quid liceat, quid deceat, quid expediat* . . . what the law permits, what equity and fairness suggest, and what will work in the situation.[2]

Each case is particular in person, time and place. To decide a case on its merits, a judge must know more than the law. He must give full consideration to one human situation in its ultimate uniqueness. The wise judge must decide what is possible and what is best, not for the Church in general, but only for the persons before him.

The canon law of the decretals was not generalized nor was it en-visioned to contain antecedently a practical answer to each particular case. It simply could not be mechanically dispensed like the printout of a programmed computer. The papal decisions were but one factor to be taken into consideration in coming to a final judgment. The conscience of the judge, his own experience and insight, and the practicality of the solution he offers to the particular problem are also vitally important. Indeed, in terms of the dynamism of the legal order itself the latter considerations are ascendant, for they feed the system from below with a constantly expanding and changing practical appraisal of lives in contemporary circumstances. We have always believed what Plato first articulated, that a wise judge will render good and just decisions even with poor laws, while an ignorant judge will render evil opinions even with the best of laws. The person of the judges, how they are appointed and to whom they are accountable is ultimately more important to a free society than the quality of particular laws. Why? Because practical wisdom in the particular case adds an indispensable, specific and interpretive element to the abstract statement of law.

The primary social purpose of the judicial process is deciding disputes in a manner that will, upon reflection, permit the loser as well as the winner to feel that he has been fairly treated. This goal requires that judges grant the parties the right to present proofs and reasoned arguments to them *and* that the judges meet the proof and reasoned arguments addressed to them by the parties.

In performing these tasks, the judges will not and should not be oblivious to what they deem are the demands of faith and an even-handed justice. All men, including judges and lawyers, are goal-oriented and can be expected to utilize all available means, including the legal system, to achieve their goals. Nevertheless, the furtherance of ecclesiastical and theological ends or the achievement of other goals through the judicial process should be secondary to its function of deciding fairly disputes between the parties who invoke it. Under this view, therefore, judges are in a position somewhat similar to that of the managers of a game who wish to make the conditions of play such that the losers as well as the winners will wish to continue to play. The fairness of the judicial process should not be sacrificed even in the name of other institutional or moral goals. Tribunals and boards of arbitration at times will be unable to pursue the particular moral goals of their judges because of the requirement that the judicial process be fair.

Almost everyone would agree that the fair disposition of disputes between the parties before the judge or the courts is an important function of the judicial process, but it is crucial to note that tribunals and commentators have not always been willing to treat it as the central social function of judicial decision-making. Judges, however, are not really guardians of the law, or of theology, or of the institutions of the Church. Guardianship is another ministry. If fairness to the parties in the resolution of their disputes is not accepted as the primary social function of the judicial process, it will be impossible to maintain that the process is objective. Moreover, one could think of better ways to resolve basic moral and theological disputes than the judicial process.

Its stylized procedures, its restricted fact-finding processes, and the limited number of parties present in any case, make it particularly ill-suited to the resolution of such broader issues.

Perhaps in more primitive times, when the tribunal and its chief administrative officer, the archdeacon, policed the morals of the community the judges were obliged to play this rôle because more adequate machinery did not exist. Today, however, the justification for such a rôle is considerably weakened. Indeed, if the resolution of the great issues of the day were the most important function of the judicial process, the tribunals would be unable to propound neutral principles; under these circumstances, the only way in which the courts could satisfy the demand for neutral principles and reasoned decisions would be to provide a comprehensive and publicly acceptable theory of the Christian life and church administration. This is surely an impossible task. Judgment based upon unspoken assumptions is always biased, because it may never be subjected to a fair criticism or rebutted. The only thing the judge can do fairly is decide each case on its merits. Impartiality must mean keeping disputes from becoming fundamental ecclesiological debates. The role of the judge is nonideological. This should be true of all judges in the Church, those of the Roman Rota and Apostolic Signatura as well as the personnel of tribunals and boards of arbitration in the local churches.

### THE JUDGE'S DECISION IS PERSONAL

Unlike other magisterial and sacramental ministries in the Church, the ministry of the judge, though it may involve an official appointment, cannot involve the articulation of a final and official ecclesiastical position. The judge's opinion will always be tentative and expressly approximative of the truth, precisely because it is so largely subjective and intended only for particular persons seeking the guidance of the judge. The judge is the master of prudence, not theology.

The personal and subjective elements in the ministry of judges are certainly recognized by the canon law, for the code itself adopts a principle of the free evaluation of evidence, common to the civil and common law traditions of the West.[3] The judge cannot decide arbitrarily before he has heard and weighed the evidence in a case and he cannot decide except upon what the evidence, the *allegata et probata*,[4] discloses.

Yet all knowledge is personal. That of a judge is no different. Michael Polanyi has said: 'The ideal of a knowledge embodied in strictly impersonal statements now appears self-contradictory, meaningless, a fit subject for ridicule. We must learn to accept as our ideal a knowledge that is manifestly personal'.[5]

The ability of a judge to distinguish important from irrelevant facts, to know that he knows enough to give a decision or to desire to pursue the inquiry further are personal skills gained only by experience. That, contrary to popular opinion, facts do not speak for themselves should be axiomatic to any student of the judicial process. The facts of a dispute, as brought forward by the briefs and record, as developed in argument, and as coming to the attention of the judge by way of judicial notice, are not themselves self-evident propositions requiring no interpretation. They exist only as contemplated by their recipient and are unavoidably colored by the reception given. As (or more) important as the facts themselves in the judicial process is the opinion based on them—the reaction they evoke in human minds. 'The assumption that events bespeak their character by merely happening has made for many strange reasonings in the history of jurisprudence. Events have meaning, it is true, but the meaning is always potential, or rather there are many meanings relative to many purposes. A situation is potentially meaningful in many directions, and which meaning is relevant is in part dependent upon a human judgment'.[6] Advocacy thus consists as much—perhaps more—of persuading the judge to take a desired view of the facts as it is of the application of law to those facts. 'To formulate the "facts" in one way and not in the other is to get one kind of decision and not another'.[7]

The point, for present purposes, is that adjudication depends as much on 'what are the facts?' as on 'what is the law?' and far more on what are the particular values at stake. Choice must be made between competing values; and choices must be made as to the interpretation to be placed on a set of 'facts'. Facts do not speak for themselves, and cannot be used by themselves for the establishment of value-judgments. As Reinhold Niebuhr puts it: 'Every judgment of fact is a judgment of value'. And as Alfred North Whitehead has told us; 'Every proposition proposing a fact must, in its complete analysis, propose the general character of the universe required for that fact. There are no self-sustained facts, floating in non-entity'.[8] Further: 'The notion of mere fact is the triumph of the abstractive intellect. It has entered into the explicit thought of no baby and of no animals . . . A single fact in isolation is the primary myth required for finite thought . . . for thought unable to embrace totality. This mythological character arises because there is no such fact. Connectedness is of the essence of things of all types. Abstraction from connectedness involves the omission of an essential factor in the fact considered. No fact is merely itself'.[9]

The point emphasized here is that there are no facts apart from a theory, and that, accordingly, a person's view of the facts is unavoidably coloured by the nature of the theory. This means that the judgment must, of its very nature, be personal. It means, furthermore, that the myth of total objectivity, that the judge merely applies a self-evident law to self-evident facts, is a cruel and misleading hoax.

### IMPARTIALITY THROUGH ACCOUNTABILITY

Impartiality in the administration of justice, the ancient ideal of justice *sine exceptione hominis,* is assured in the Church, not by denying the undeniably personal component in the judge's practical ability to decide, but rather in strictly adhering to procedures to make judges accountable for decisions to their own consciences, to the parties before them and to the Church. In effect, what this means is that the Church demands of judges a reasoned opinion. Developing reasons and writing them down as a logical *apologia* for decisions is only secondarily required by the canons to permit the possibility of appeal.[10] It is primarily mandated as a check against arbitrariness and capriciousness, which is, of course, the tyranny of man over man. This is a variation of a principle of the reasonableness of law, that justice is not really done until it is seen to be done.

The classical expression of the appeal to the judge's conscience as a check against arbitrariness comes from Pope Innocent III. The judge, he said, must always bear in mind that he himself is subject to the judgment of God; he must give judgment *solum Deum prae oculis habens.*[11] This, of course, means that he cannot merely consider the letter of the law. He must honestly evaluate the evidence before him. It also means that the right of appeal in the Church always lies against an opinion that is alleged to be whimsical or capricious. 'For the love of justice', Pope Alexander III said, 'one should judge with an eye upon God'.[12] This principle is so strong that in cases of conflict between the demands of the law and what the judge believes to be true, the majority opinion of the canonists is that the conscience of the judge must prevail.[13] 'It is better to permit scandal', the rule of law says, 'than to abandon the truth'.[14] The canon law is very clear about the judge's accountability to his conscience.

The canons are less clear, however, about the judge's duty to give reasons for his decisions to the parties who invoke them. They are totally silent, and deliberately so to foster confidentiality, about the accountability of the judges to the faithful in local communities concerned about decisions that affect them. These are defects in the present law easily overlooked in a paternalistic age, but poisonous to the ministry of judges at this time. There are several reasons why peremptory decisions are self-defeating.

The first is that the reassurance of impartiality and security in judgment demand some reasonably objective means for determining how to proceed from the objectively-given reference points of the judicial process—the canons and the known decisions in previous cases—to the decision of new cases. In terms of social function that we have posited for the legal system, only such a claim of objectivity will make it possible for the losers in the judicial forum to feel that they have been fairly treated. As we have noted, fairness requires that a party before a judicial tribunal be permitted to present proofs and arguments and that the tribunal's decision meet these proofs and arguments. Beyond this minimum, we are obliged to provide criteria which, if we are speaking in terms of 'fairness', will permit us to say that the proofs and arguments of the parties have been adequately met and which, if we are speaking in terms of 'objectivity,' will permit us to say that a case has been properly decided. Without such criteria, a disappointed litigant cannot be criticized if he refuses to acknowledge the objective character of the judicial process and if he claims that the court's statements about his arguments are only window-dressing and that his participation in the process was merely a charade.

A judge should be free to decide a case in a manner different from that of the decided cases arising on the same grounds only if he can point to a significant factual difference between the instant case and previously decided cases. A loser in court can only be assured of justice if he can be led to understand the legal reasons the judge used in deciding his case and what precisely was the significance of the difference the judge found between this case and other cases that were decided differently, under which he argued.

The single, most important reason for a lack of faith in the objectivity of the tribunals is that with the present procedures it is practically impossible for the faithful to understand what the tribunals are doing or why they decide as they do. A reasoned decision is surely required by canon law, but it is required only at the conclusion of a formal process.[15] Most tribunals do almost anything to avoid a formal process. The vast majority of petitioners come to the tribunals, pour out their souls about the most intimate details of a marriage long dead and then simply hear no more for months or years. Finally, a letter comes to tell them nothing can be done, or that the case has been sent to Rome or that they should go to their pastor to have their present marriage blessed or that some further evidence is needed. Have they really had the benefit of a judicial process? Not by any means. After an interminable wait they have either been screened out by the so-called 'preliminary investigation' or their case has been sent through administrative channels. In either case the judges have avoided the onus of reasoned decision. The faithful are elated or dejected, in either case without knowing why and in an adverse case without the slightest hope of appeal. This kind of nonsense is a mockery of justice. To make a judgment on the merits of a case means, if nothing else, that the merits be clearly and understandably articulated. Judges must be accountable to the persons who come before them to give them a full explanation of their decisions.

## A RESOURCE OF PRACTICAL WISDOM

A final word should be said about the accountability of the judge to the Church, not as a check upon his discretion, but rather as a contribution to the pastoral guidance of the faithful. No case is decided in a vacuum. No decision is reached without struggle, without a creative effort, without effect upon persons who come later. In trying cases judges try the law itself, interpret it and gradually change it. The changes they make are interstitial, in the gaps and lacunae. Gradually exceptions become rules, gaps are filled, new knowledge renders old maxims incomplete and new standards are born. The changes the judges make are so important that their opinions should be kept and circulated, tested by scholars and pastors, refined further by the experience of the faithful and eventually more fully articulated in legislation. The work of judges lends dynamism and life to the law. One need only to reflect upon the efforts of judges in elaborating theories of capacity to marry, discretion and interpersonal psychology in the recent jurisprudence of the Rota to see the significance of the creative rôle of the judges in the Church.[16] This creative role should be officially recognized and expanded from Rome to the local churches, from tribunals to committees of arbitration and conciliation by the circulation of widely reported opinions.

Scholarly criticism of the judicial process has been abundant and wide-ranging in legal literature for the past two generations.[17] Since the publication in 1899 of François Gény's *Methode d'Interpretation et Sources en Droit Privé Positif* a consensus has grown to become universal that judges have a creative role in law. It is no longer a matter of serious controversy that in any working legal system the judiciary plays a major part in the evolution of law. This represents an essential breakthrough from a conceptualism which, in the civilian world dominated by the French Code Civil, regarded the process of judicial interpretation as a logical analytical process of subsumption, and in the common law world regarded the application of precedent to the case at hand equally a process of analytical—though inductive—reasoning. A great deal of judge-made law, however, begins not with reason, but with intuition, with the psychological realities of a given situation. Judges must delicately balance interests and weigh values in practical decisions. This continuous evaluative process leads to the refining of skills that become the distinctive mark of the judicial temperament. The truly great jurist who has borne the lonely burden of responsible choice, the *nobile officium* of judge, for many years gradually becomes a person of almost inestimable value for society. His is a strength of mind that gives confidence, an insight into human affairs that penetrates the secrets of hearts, a patience that inspires peace and a respect for persons that calms and heals the wounded. The great jurist is not forgotten. His use of law for persons creates a living justice; it is truly a charism, the *ars boni et aequi*. This without doubt is a treasured creative ministry to be prized in all the judges of the Church.

## CONCLUSION

For a judge to decide each case upon its own merits requires a fierce self-discipline and a continuous effort to grow in insight and impartiality. The struggle itself is a service to mankind; its fruit is the grace of a truly healing ministry. We have discussed a revitalization of the office of judge in the Church. The principles expressed are applicable in all forms of formal and informal decision-making wherein choice is particularized to the merits of a single case. Let us not forget that those who bear the burden of such choice in the context of faith are in the Christian tradition among the most honoured in our midst.

## Notes

1. Potthast, *Regesta Pontificum Romanorum* (Berol. 1873), no. 9694: Spoleto, Sept. 5, 1234.
2. *Lib. Dec. Grego. IX, cap. Magnae devotionis,* 7, X, 3,34: Rome, The Lateran, March 1198.
3. Canon 1869 (CIC) accepts in principle that the judge must ultimately be free to make up his own mind in evaluating evidence laid before him. The 1917 Code borrowed this principle from civil law. See Heinrich Flatten, "Qua libertate iudex ecclesiasticus probationes appretiare possit et debeat," *Apollinaris* (1960), pp. 182–210 (previously in German, in *Tübinger Theologische Quartalschrift,* 139 [1959], pp. 427–60).
4. 'Ecclesia in suo regimine ab arbitrio abhorret, in quo praesumptio odii vel calumniae plerumque non deerit.' S. R. Rota, *Cincinnaten., Translationis,* 16 July 1912, c. R.P.D. Prior, vol. IV, Dec. XXX, n. 6, p. 355.
5. M. Polanyi, *The Study of Man* (London, 1958), p. 27.

6. J. Garlan, *Legal Realism and Justice* (New York, 1941), p. 31.

7. *Idem.*, p. 38.

8. A. N. Whitehead, *Process and Reality* (New York, 1929), p. 17.

9. A. N. Whitehead, *Modes of Thought* (New York, 1938), pp. 12–3.

10. Canons 1840, §3; 1874, §4; 1875, 1894 (CIC). This is in accord with the civil law. See Article III of the Constitution of the Italian Republic: 'All jurisdictional decisions must be motivated.'

11. Pope Innocent III, *cap. Qualiter et quando*, 17, X, 5, 1, *De Accusationibus*. With this rule Franz Schmalzgrueber, one of the greatest of the Church's jurists, begins his treatise on the office of judge in the Church. *Ius Canonicum Universum*, Lib. I, Pars I, *Regula iudicis ecclesiastici* (Romae, 1843), p. 167. Isidore of Seville says precisely: 'Qui Dei iudicia oculis suis proposuit, semper timens et tremens in omni negotio formidat, ne de iustitiae tramite cadat; et unde non iustificatur, inde potius condemnetur'. Can. *Omnis*, 10 Dist. XLV, *S. Isidori Sententiarum*, lib. III, cap. 52, n. 4.

12. Pope Alexander III, *cap. Ex parte*, 7, X, 2, 20, *De testibus et attestationibus*.

13. Pope Innocent III, *cap. Pastoralis*, 28, X, I, 29, *De officio et potestate iudicis*. In this regard, see J. Delanglade, 'Le juge, serviteur de la loi ou gardien de la justice selon la tradition théologique', *Revue de Droit Canonique* (1960), pp. 141–64, (1961), pp. 3–31.

14. *Reg. Iuris*, cap. 3: '. . . utilius scandalum nasci permittitur quam veritas deseratur'.

15. Canons 1874 and 1877 (C.I.C.).

16. Pope Paul VI discussed the creative rôle of the judges of the Roman Rota in an important address to its auditors and staff several years ago. See Discourse to the Rota, Feb. 8, 1973. *A.A.S.* 65 (1973), pp. 95–103.

17. This vast subject can be surveyed in M. Taruffo, *La Motivazione della Sentenza Civile* (Padua, 1975); R. Wasserstrom, *The Judicial Decision* (Stanford, 1961); R. Sprung, Ed., *Entscheidungsbegrundung* (Vienna, 1974); or C. Perelman, 'Droit, philosophie et argumentation', in *Handlingen van de vereniging voor wijsbegeerte des rechts*, LV (1971). In the literature of canon law a very good study of the rôle of judge using traditional sources is that of Cardinal André Jullien, *Juges et avocats des tribunaux de l'Église* (Rome, 1970).

Hans Heimerl

# Arbitration and Reconciliation in Church Disputes

THE TREND TOWARDS ARBITRATION

IN recent years increasing attempts have been made to find new ways
of solving legal conflict within the church. People are no longer content
to have disputes solved by church officials or their superiors and an
appeal to the traditional ecclesiastical courts is rarely taken into consideration. Indeed, why have the conflict settled by a sovereign authority at all? Could this not be achieved by arbitration? Better still, the
conflict should be set straight by means of amicable agreement at the
earliest stage possible. This kind of approach has occasionally been
translated into institutional terms. It does however make for a certain
lack of clarity as regards limits, classification and internal structure.

Attempts at mediation or even an official arbitration office have come
into force before the establishment of the planned ecclesiastical courts
of administration.[1] In some dioceses arbitration offices have already
been established. As neutral mediators these offices are able to put
forward various possible solutions to the parties concerned or if both
parties agree, they can act as courts of arbitration and make decisions
that are legally binding. These organizations are explicitly designed to
deal with disputes between individuals and large bodies of authorities.[2]
Judicial questions arising from the establishment of new committees
such as the pastoral council, the priests' council or the council of the
laity will gladly be referred to the newly formed courts of arbitration.
Employment disputes would also be handled by the arbitration offices
acting in accordance with the state legal system. Should the decisions

69

reached by these "courts of arbitration" be thought to have been in any way forced, they will be referred to the bishop for affirmation.[3] To cope with legal issues of this kind it would be more appropriate for bishops to create special advisory committees to ensure that justice is done; these would assist the bishops in their decision making, but could also be appealed to by the parties concerned as a court of arbitration.[4] Attempts are also being made to link all these different elements in a single institution.[5]

The causes of these new developments are to some extent easily identifiable, though in other respects they are less obvious. The various committees set up by the second Vatican Council were largely unknown in traditional canon law. The latter's relationship to individual officials, the procedure for electing members, the extent of their competence and control over the legality of their actions are all as yet unresolved issues. It should be noted that under civil law special courts are set up or expert arbitrators called in to deal with specialized subject matter. The church would seem to be proceeding in a similar manner.

Conflict between the individual and society, between the member of the church and the hierarchy is by no means new. But in recent years the individual in the church has become more aware of his own merits and autonomy. Relations between individuals and officers of the church are no longer seen merely in terms of subordination and superiority, but as a partnership. Previously, complaints were dealt with as a matter of course by the sovereign administrative body with an important official acting as mediator. Nowadays, however, justice or even an 'act of grace' is not so frequently sought 'from above'. There is a desire to solve disagreements by means of straightforward discussions between the individuals concerned and with the help of the decisions of independent courts, or better still by means of non-authoritarian mediators.

The inadequacy of existing ecclesiastical courts is repeatedly cited as the cause of these developments. These courts devote virtually all their time to marriage cases and their procedures are too impractical and tedious to solve the controversies continually arising within the sphere of ecclesiastical administration; indeed, most of them would not be competent to deal with such matters.

The anti-juridical bias prevailing in the church today may be partly responsible for this desire to bypass the ecclesiastical courts and their formalized legal procedures. Strangely enough, there is a tendency in this search for new ways of solving conflicts to rely on models from the state system.

The decisive factors are: to bear in mind the genuine Christian approach of becoming reconciled before it reaches the stage of legal proceedings (Mt 5:25); the command to set one's brother right if he has sinned (Mt 18:15ff.); and to remember the example of the New Testament communities. Even canon lawyers realize that the most important characteristic of our jurisdiction is the harmonious solution of legal differences.[6] Bishops are bound to prevent the proceedings going any further than necessary by making a doctrinal protest and by referring those concerned to the gospel precedent.[7]

Christianity came into being in a Roman and Jewish environment which was well-disposed towards the system of arbitration. Like the Jews a minority group in a pagan state, the Christian communities did not wish to settle their internal conflicts in pagan courts. They were even more strongly aware of the command to avoid quarrels altogether, but rather to suffer wrong (1 Cor 6:1–8). Under Constantine, the Roman state found this espiscopal arbitration so indispensable that it could not be revoked by a civil judge. Shortly afterwards arbitration by a bishop was recognized as valid by the state even if only requested by one party. The final step had been taken from arbitrator to judge.

### A SYSTEMATIC EXAMINATION

*1. Compulsory courts of arbitration* and compulsory attempts to reach a settlement are based on historical precedent, yet they lack that essential element of reconciliation, namely that they should be voluntary. They have nothing in common with the established code of the Latin church.[8] However, failure to participate in an attempt to reach a settlement organized by a special office legally instituted for that purpose resulted in the forfeiture of the individual's right of appeal to the administrative court. Courts of arbitration are declared competent to deal with specific issues, e.g. those connected with post-conciliar committees, complaints against the church administration or civil disputes. The decisions of these courts of arbitration are valid even if both parties do not freely submit to them; nor may the parties wholly determine who sits on these courts.

Bearing in mind that such courts of arbitration and procedures for reaching a settlement out of court are based not only on the principle of harmonious agreement, but also resort to compulsory rulings in matters of civil controversy, they can hardly be said to live up to their name. Nevertheless, they do possess several qualities inherent to the process of arbitration or settlement. The parties are not infrequently given the right to participate in the selection of the board of arbitrators, which means that they may nominate one of the arbitrators. Even the aim of official settlements is not merely to establish truth and justice but to achieve a harmonious solution based on agreement and compromise. Most important of all, this procedure avoids the formalism and unwieldiness of the traditional legal system.

Given all these features linking them with the civil courts of arbitration, these informal settlement procedures and courts of arbitration with their powers of compulsion should be given a recognized function in the church. Furthermore, the characteristically informal nature of the court of arbitration cannot be maintained when dealing with the actions and rights of public bodies or church officials. Ecclesiastical courts of arbitration will frankly not be of much use if the plaintiff is able to appeal to a state court instead (e.g., in cases connected with employment).

Despite the special nature of ecclesiastical courts of arbitration with compulsory powers there is still a case for their being properly and systematically organized. They must either be genuine courts of arbitration and settlement bringing about unconditional agreement between the parties; or alternatively, they must be conceived and designated as special courts or administrative bodies. The best solution of all would be for the church's legal system to be more understanding towards the need for such courts of arbitration.

*2. Arbitration on a voluntary basis.* For a harmonious solution to be reached, the dissenting parties must contractually agree to bypass the public courts and to entrust the decision to one or more arbitrators. Hence the actual decision is not reached unanimously by the parties concerned; however, by agreeing to place the matter in the hands of arbitrators they have already taken the first step towards reconciliation, which indirectly includes the dispute itself.

Under established canon law[9] arbitrators may be instructed to make a decision strictly in keeping with the law (as 'arbitri') or simply according to what they think right and fitting (as 'arbitratores'). In the latter case there is already an element of reconciliation involved. Nevertheless these 'arbitratores' are able to reach a binding decision because of the arbitration contract drawn up between the parties. In cases of arbitration, canon law adopts the relevant civil law, which has the advantage that the final decision is valid from both the ecclesiastical and the civil points of view. In areas where the stipulations of civil law are too complex for the court of arbitration to handle, its application to ecclesiastical issues is likewise limited. The alternative is to appeal to a court of equity (arbitratores) if the latter is not controlled by the state legal system.

The typical instance where arbitration is used, namely in legal disputes between two individuals concerning ecclesiastical issues, is very rare. But can arbitration be used to solve the much more frequent controversies between an individual member of the church and a church official or institution, or even between two ecclesiastical institutions? Objections can be raised against this proposal, on the grounds that the arbitration contract is of a personal legal nature and that the grounds for dispute are no longer in the hands of the parties concerned, and hence excluded from arbitration or settlement. Arbitration would be possible in circumstances where two ecclesiastical institutions of equal standing were involved, for example, two parish priests or a diocese and a religious order. However, where the controversy is between an official representative of the church in his official capacity and some inferior person or body, in other words in disputes of an administrative nature, private arbitration would clearly not be admissible. But the competent authority (in the case of a diocese, the bishop) may delegate the arbitrators chosen by the dissenting parties to make a decision on his behalf, on condition that they adhere to certain forms of arbitration. A 'court of arbitration' of this kind would, by its very nature, no longer fulfil its original function. Instead, it would become an administrative body, though retaining some of the decisive features of the court of arbitration such as voluntary agreement, a simpler procedure and a certain degree of independence (if the official in charge is trustworthy and genuinely refrains from abusing his authority).

The arbitration system is caught up in the tension between the painstaking legal exatitude and unwieldiness of the ordinary courts and its own flexibility of procedure and principles of justice, which might lead to accusations that it is not objective enough. Its chance lies in a compromise between these two extremes.

3. *Mediation (arbitration)*. Unlike the arbitrator himself, the mediator in a legal dispute is not involved in decision-making. His sole concern is to help the parties to reach an agreement among themselves, either by persuading them to enter into negotiations, or by putting forward suggestions for a solution. There are various different methods which can be used to solve disputes, all of which must be considered. They are: a privately drawn up legal contract; a settlement; a unilateral action conceded by the opposing party; and a civil action complying with the wishes of a plaintiff appealing against a previous court ruling. On the whole, a solution will represent a compromise, but it can also correspond more closely to the standpoint of one or the other of the parties concerned; a further possibility is that it will consist of the most objective acknowledgment and evaluation of the legal situation.

Hence mediation can be used in a far wider number of cases and is even more flexible than the system of arbitration, in that it attempts to effect a direct reconciliation between the parties.

Mediation is also found in institutionalized form in established canon law[10] as the attempt at reconciliation proposed by the judge. However, once a case has been taken to court the plaintiff is usually determined to pursue legal proceedings, so any attempt to mediate at this stage is generally too late. Anyone who feels his rights have been infringed will seek the simplest way to vindicate himself. If mediation were presented to him along these lines as a convincing means of reaching an amiable solution, he would doubtless try it. Hence the efforts to offer an institutionalized way of reaching a settlement without going to court. This is the function of the diocesan organizations recently set up for the express purpose of mediating in legal disputes.

The unanimity aimed at by these means will often represent a compromise which does not necessarily correspond to objective truth or absolute justice. But given the fact that the whole truth and absolute justice are ideals scarcely attainable in this world, a peace compromise can be considered acceptable. However, the danger of a compromise is that it favours the stronger of the two parties and that it frustrates the individual's demand for justice. Hence in addition to the friendly settlement that can be brought about by arbitration, the option to pursue justice through the courts must also remain open, not just legally, but in practice. The church should promote organizations that can bring about reconciliation where possible, but it also needs to reform its legal system.

Essentially, the rules that apply in the case of an amicable settlement achieved without the help of a mediator are the same as those used in arbitration. But it is often more difficult to make the first step towards the opponent than towards an impartial mediator.

*4. Pastoral and psychological advice?* In certain circumstances both courts and reconciliation boards are obviously able to give legal advice and thus often succeed in avoiding legal disputes. Intensive legal advice is, it is true, left to the canon lawyers.

Legal problems very often have a psychological cause, whether individual or sociological. Personal tensions find an outlet in legal quarrels; an inferiority complex can make an individual very conscious of having suffered an injustice. A wide variety of tensions between church officials and ordinary members of the laity are settled by administrative measures. The generation problem, symbolized by a clinging to tradition and a lack of understanding for reforms, also manifests itself in legal disputes. To acknowledge and solve the problems of interaction and communication underlying all this would seem to be the simplest way of settling disputes. The provision already made in the church for individual psychological advice, in addition to those projects now being devised, can help a great deal. Pastoral institutions and church officials are striving to avoid and overcome conflict within the community of the church.

However helpful and underrated the contribution of pastoral work and psychological advice in the problem of solving conflicts, they can never replace or supplant justice. Still less should they serve ecclesiastical legislators as an excuse for not providing effective protection for the rights of the individual.

### SOME REMARKS ON FUTURE DEVELOPMENT

The apparatus for bringing about reconciliation in legal disputes has not been in existence for long enough in the Catholic Church for us to be able to draw any definitive conclusions. Periodic observations would seem to confirm the experience of the long-established arbitration boards organized by the Evangelical Church in Germany: namely, that they are rarely used. Problematic situations are apparently dealt with by other means. We can only guess at the reasons for this phenomenon. It may be that the arbitration boards seem too like another new church institution enjoying compulsory powers. In short, too far removed from everyday reality. It is also possible that they are not taken very seriously by the church officials who set them up in the first place.[11] On the other hand, other reports indicate just the reverse, that arbitration boards and conciliation offices are called upon regularly and make an important contribution towards solving legal disputes.

The desire for rapid, effective and readily available assistance and amicable agreement is there. If this desire is to be fulfilled, the machinery for legal reconciliation must be as flexible as possible and contain the minimum legal structure and procedure. It rests with individuals to make use of it and its suggestions of their own free will. Other functions should be left to other, possibly existing bodies (courts, administrative authorities). The personal closeness and familiarity that exists in a diocese, and would be a disadvantage for a diocesan administrative court, could be a distinct advantage for a diocesan arbitration board conceived along these lines. It would obviously have to be composed of persons trusted by all sides. Whether there exists a need for permanent legal arbitration at a higher level, for instance within the framework of a bishops' conference, or whether ad hoc mediators or arbitrators are sufficient, remains to be seen.

The ultimate aim is to promote rather than to institutionalize the central factor on which it all depends: the desire for reconciliation demanded of us by Christ.

*Translated by Sarah Twohig*

## Notes

1. 'Kirchliche Verwaltungsprozessordnung der Kirchenprovinzen in Bayern, Entwurf 1971', *Periodica* 60 (1971), p. 620 (Art. 28); K. Ludicke, 'Chancen einer kirchlichen Verwaltungsgerichtsbarkeit', *Herder-Korr.* 28 (1974), p. 308; W. Geiger, 'Probleme kirchliche Verwaltungsgerichtsbarkeit' *Internat. kath. Zeitschr.* 2 (1973), pp. 269–83. Cf. also P. Huizing in *Concilium* 7 (1971).

2. Cf. 'Kirchliche Schlichtungsinstanzen in den USA?' *Herder-Korr.* 24 (1970) pp. 11 ff.

3. H. Krätzl, 'Pastorale Schiedsgerichte in der Erzdiözese Wien', *Theol.-prakt. Quartalscher.* 122 (1974), pp. 244ff., K. T. Geringer, 'Die sogenannten Schiedsgerichte in der Erzdiözese Wien', *Arch. f. kath. Kirchenrecht* 142 (1973), pp. 436–54.

4. V. Rovera, 'Episcopi "sacrum ius . . ." de opportunitate instituendi Consilium diocesanum iustitiae', *Periodica* 20 (1971), pp. 573–90.

5. 'Statuten der Schichtungs- und Schiedsstellen österreichischer Diözesen', *Arch. f. kath. Kirchenrecht* 142 (1973), pp. 499 ff.; 143 (1974), pp. 490 ff. *Österreichischer Synodaler Vorgang,* Documents (Vienna, 1974), pp. 31, 35, 45 f.

6. P. Wesemann, 'Ad Tuenda Iura Personarum', *Diaconia et ius* (Munich, 1973), p. 159.

7. J. Neumann, *Menschenrechte auch in der Kirche?* (Zurich, 1976), p. 158.

8. E. Melichar, 'Das schiedsrichterliche Verfahren im kanonischen Recht', *Österr. Arch. f. Kirchenrecht* 2 (1951), p. 197.

9. Can. 1929 (C.I.C.).

10. Can. 1925 (C. I. C.).

11. Cf. Neumann, *op. cit.*, pp. 176 f.

Francis Morrisey

# The Procedural and Administrative Reforms of the Post-Conciliar Church

A study of post-conciliar writings on various aspects of Church life shows that reference is made on occasion to such expressions as 'subsidiarity', 'collegiality', 'participation', and so forth. These terms are used in various senses, without any definition being assigned. To understand their meaning, it is necessary to return to the sources of the expression in the conciliar texts.

For instance, the Council used the word 'subsidiarity' on three occasions[1] assigning different meanings to the term: recourse to outside authorities to compensate for a deficiency in a subordinate body, leaving to these subordinate bodies the right to make decisions that can aptly be taken at their level, and, decentralization of authority and power. The same applies to the term 'collegiality' which is now used to describe not only the rôle of the bishops acting as a body, but also the process whereby many people cooperate together to promote the common good.

These two realities—or better, attitudes—which have come down from the Council, find their application in different areas of life. However, one sector where they might be applied effectively is that of court judgments and procedures by allowing local tribunals to make decisions that can be executed immediately, and by authorizing the bishops of a region or territory to devise procedural norms corresponding to the sensitivities of the area while still protecting the basic rights of the faithful to have their status recognized by law.

The need for decentralization and of having better adapted procedural norms has become increasingly evident in the last decade. A growing number of cases have been before the courts. While most of these are concerned with declarations of nullity of marriage, there are a surprising number of instances involving conflicts of rights now being settled by administrative tribunals and 'due process' boards.

In addition to decentralization and flexibility of norms, we also find it necessary to infuse a new spirit into our present procedural legislation. For this, we take our inspiration from Paul VI himself who, when speaking on January 28, 1971, to the personnel of the Sacred Roman Rota, drew the attention of his listeners to the fact that 'it is unfortunately true that the Church, in the exercise of her power . . . has in the course of the centuries borrowed from civil legislators certain serious imperfections, even methods which were unjust in the true and proper sense, at least objectively speaking'.[2] This recognition of the fact that there are injustices or unjust methods in the exercise of the judicial power has incited many canonists to spare no effort to try and have them removed, once they have been identified appropriately. But the Holy Father, on other occasions, goes even further in drawing attention to these deficiencies. Indeed, since he has become Pope, Paul VI has repeated his intention to have ecclesial law based on doctrine so that it could 'deepen the work of the Spirit',[3] and not be simply a reflection of the civil law of a given country.

Thus, keeping these four points in mind: need of decentralization, flexibility of norms, removal of injustices, preparation of a law based on doctrine and not modelled on a particular legislative system, I shall try to review some of the major changes that have been introduced in procedural law since the second Vatican Council. I shall then examine the drafts of the proposed new procedural law. In a third part, I intend to consider three particular situations in law which must be faced today. Finally, I shall present some personal suggestions for a further revision of the existing legislation. It goes without saying that the scope of the present study does not afford the luxury of an in-depth examination of the various topics to be treated.

### CHANGES IN PROCEDURAL LAW SINCE THE SECOND VATICAN COUNCIL

On a number of occasions since the conclusion of the second Vatican Council, the procedural laws of the Church have been revised, either for the Church as a whole, or for particular countries or territories. We shall briefly review these different revisions, indicating their particular characteristics.

1. The Motu proprio "De Episcoporum muneribus" of June 15, 1966, concerning the dispensing power of bishops, explicitly removed

procedural laws from this power 'since they are established for the defense of rights, and dispensation from them does not concern the spiritual good of the faithful.'[4] It is clear then that such legislation is beyond the scope of the bishop's dispensing power. Consequently, since the Council—as before—the bishops have not been authorized to dispense or derogate from the general norms of the Church in this regard.

2. The Apostolic Constitution *Regimini Ecclesiae Universae*, August 15, 1967, transferred from the Sacred Congregation for Sacraments to the Supreme Tribunal of the Apostolic Signatura the supervision of the correct administration of justice.[5] Henceforth, norms regarding procedures and tribunals are normally to be issued by this body.

The same Constitution also established a second section of the Apostolic Signatura, which would serve as an administrative tribunal and provide redress against abuses once other means had been exhausted. This was a very important innovation which had beneficial repercussions in many instances.

3. On April 28, 1970, the Council for the Public Affairs of the Church authorized the use of provisional norms for marriage cases in the United States of America.[6] Known as the 'American Procedural Norms', they were renewed in 1973 and again in 1974 when they were extended on an indefinite basis, that is, until the new law on procedure comes into effect. In the same period, revised norms were granted to the Episcopal Conferences of Australia, Belgium, England and Wales. Special norms were also issued for Canada in 1974.

This granting of particular norms was certainly an important step in the revision of procedural law. It responded to the presentations made by Episcopal Conferences and enabled the bishops to adapt the general norms of the Church to particular needs of certain areas, introducing a form of decentralization in the process.

4. On December 28, 1970, the Apostolic Signatura issued a circular letter and norms regarding interdiocesan, regional or inter-regional tribunals,[7] 'not with the intent of referring everything to itself alone',[8] but to assist the courts throughout the Church. These norms recommended the unification of diocesan tribunals where possible to provide for better and more qualified service. At the same time, the Apostolic Signatura reserved the right to have the courts forward to its offices copies of their decisions for revision.

There are positive and negative aspects to this document. A regional tribunal is certainly a good exercise in collegiality; it generally provides for a more qualified dispensation of justice and its findings are of assistance to other courts. On the other hand, though, this same document centralizes to a great extent all tribunal matters in the Apostolic

Signatura, leaving almost no room for individuality or adaptation to local customs. Likewise, when this supreme Tribunal proceeds in an exclusively judicial manner, it risks perpetuating some of the civil law formalities alluded to earlier.

5. Many important changes in the general procedural law of the Church in the post-conciliar era were incorporated into the Motu proprio *Causas matrimoniales* of March 28, 1971.[9] This document modifies a number of prescriptions of the universal law, the most significant of which was the simplification of procedures for appeals in marriage nullity cases. The new law also extended some of the grounds of competence of courts, enabling the tribunals to handle cases more expeditiously.

It was hoped that this document would satisfy those who were calling for a simplification of norms. However, the result was not exactly as expected. While gratefully receiving the simplifications given, many episcopal conferences wanted to have the mandatory second instance decision eliminated in all cases.

Likewise, since the publication of the Motu proprio, a number of restrictive interpretations have been issued or given, thus removing even some of the simplifications that the new law might have contained.[10]

6. On October 30, 1971, the Secretariate of State authorized the use of 'due process' or conciliation and arbitration norms in the United States of America.[11] Similar norms were also considered for Bavaria.[12] This document was eventually to serve as a basis for the establishment of a new sub-commission within the Pontifical Commission for the Revision of the Code of Canon Law, to study administrative procedures in the Church. The 'due process' document enabled persons who wished to avail themselves of its norms to follow an accurate yet uncomplicated procedure to resolve differences, without having to become involved in lengthy and costly tribunal procedures.

7. Further procedural changes were introduced by the Instruction *Dispensationis matrimonii rati* of the S.C. for the Discipline of the Sacraments, March 7, 1972.[13] This document, while referring specifically to cases of non-consummation of marriage, introduced significant changes regarding the use of mechanical means of recording, credibility witnesses, and so forth; likewise, by authorizing diocesan bishops to begin the study of such cases on their own initiative, it provided a further instance of simplification and decentralization.

8. The Motu proprio *Cum matrimonialium* of September 8, 1973,[14] extends to the Oriental churches the major prescriptions of *Causas* of an interposed appeal or recourse'[19] has already proven its value and

9. The final document to date which incorporates legislative changes in the universal procedural law, is the Instruction and Norms of De-

cember 6, 1973, issued by the S.C. for the Doctrine of Faith, regarding Privilege of the Faith cases.[15]

These legislative texts, issued over a ten-year period, attempt to meet the need for a simplification of tribunal procedures in the Church. However, they proceeded in a piecemeal fashion, without undertaking a general review or study of the legislation as a whole. This was to be the task of the Commission for Revision of the Code which was entrusted with the task of preparing new procedural legislation for the universal Church. Let us now examine the results of its work to date.

## PROPOSED CHANGES IN PROCEDURAL LAW

Two documents have been distributed to date by the Commission for the Revision of the Code which are directly related to the question of procedural law. The first, sent to the episcopal conferences in 1972, presented the text of 26 canons on administrative procedure.[16] The second, dated November 3, 1976, proposed some 449 canons (including 39 on administrative procedure).[17] Let us refer briefly to each of these texts.

## 1. Administrative Procedure

Shortly after the approval of the 'due process' norms for the United States of America in 1971, the bishops received the text of the proposed new procedure to be followed in cases where it was felt that the rights of persons were being infringed upon. One or more administrative tribunals could be established in the territory of each conference to study appeals against decisions given by persons in authority, but in an extra-judicial context.

If this document is approved and promulgated, it will compensate for a serious deficiency in the current Church law, which, for all practical purposes, provided little redress against what could be arbitrary decisions of ecclesiastical authorities.

## 2. Formal Procedure

The second document, distributed in late 1976, seems to constitute a backwards step in procedural legislation. It presents a proposed new law which would revise the present Book IV of the Code of Canon Law. While taking into account most of the simplifications authorized by *Causas matrimoniales,* it fails to account for the content of the particular indults granted in recent years to various Episcopal Conferences.

The draft would retain almost exclusively the civil law perspective of the Code, with little or no reference to the doctrinal foundation of the law itself. For instance, marriage cases would still be presented in the context of contentious cases, where there is a conflict of rights, while, in practice, in the vast majority of cases, there is no conflict of rights, but only a desire to receive a declaration of nullity if, in fact, the marriage was invalid.

The document does not provide that access to tribunal positions of importance be open to women. Influenced probably by the civil law of some countries, canons would be added concerning custody of children, and the continuation of cases after the death of one of the parties. Likewise, the validity of decisions would still depend to a large extent on the validity of prescribed acts of the process and of the accompanying documents.

This does not mean that there are not positive points in the schema. Indeed, there are: a reversal of the order of proofs by admitting documentary evidence (such as medical reports) as having priority over the statements of witnesses, equality between the Defender of the Bond and the Advocate, possibility of oral discussion of cases, sanation of procedural defects by the sentence, and so forth. But these are probably only details in an overall picture.

The principle of subsidiarity, in the sense of decentralization, is almost non-existent in the draft text. Indeed, very little is left to the bishops' conferences to decide. The procedure is highly centralized because of the possibility of eventual appeals to Rome against decisions of lower courts. It could reasonably be presumed that there will be opposition to the document in many countries because it does not incorporate the content of indults already granted. This is regrettable, because if the new Code of Canon Law, when it is promulgated, is considered to be out of touch with reality, the credibility of the Church as a whole will suffer since its law will not conform to the declarations and policies of its leaders, and will not meet the needs of the times. It is to be sincerely hoped that serious effort will be made to have the draft radically revised so that it will correspond better to the thrust that we have come to expect in the Church and its pronouncements.

### APPLICATIONS OF THE PRINCIPLES OF THE RENEWED PROCEDURAL LAW

A procedural law will be good law in as much as it is able to fulfill its role: the protection of rights. The moment law becomes a serious obstacle to this end, it must be reexamined and reevaluated. There are a number of instances today where, it seems, the procedural law as we have it, is not able to fulfill its specific role, or can only do so with great difficulty. Let us examine three of these cases.

## 1. Moral Certitude

In a well-publicized address to the Sacred Roman Rota on October 1, 1942, Pius XII considered at length the question of moral certitude and the conflict that could arise when a judge feels that 'he has moral certainty regarding the truth of the fact at issue, while at the same time, in his capacity as judge, he denies the same objective certainty on the basis of procedural law'.[18] Pius XII said that such a conflict was not admissible, but that the judge should undertake a further and more accurate examination of the case. This is a point that today is still causing difficulties. We are still faced with two extremes: a slavish following of procedural norms, or a complete disregard of them. Certainly, the answer lies somewhere between the two. The observance of the norms of law is a guarantee against arbitrary and capricious decisions, a value that the Church does not intend to disregard. But, the question may be asked whether there are not other ways of protecting people's rights.

The greater recognition given to moral certitude means that courts must be able to continue to seek new procedural solutions to difficult cases, such as the application of the norms regarding citation of a respondent whose whereabouts are completely unknown, accepting cases where there is no proof other than the statements of the plaintiff who is credible, the study of cases when existing medical documentation is not released, or when witnesses refuse to cooperate.

A renewed understanding of these laws is becoming part of procedural practice in courts today, even though the law itself has not recognized the facts formally.

## 2. Non-judicial Decisions

We are also faced today with a very serious problem: the large number of non-judicial or 'good conscience' solutions being given to cases either when it is impossible to have a judicial decision, or when people choose to ignore the prescribed formalities. Undoubtedly, there are many instances when it is almost impossible to obtain a judicial decision, but the growing number of cases resolved in this manner is indicative of a very serious situation.

If the bishops of various regions were authorized to prepare procedural norms that could be applied appropriately in their own territories, we might be able to overcome some of the obstacles hindering us today and would thus be able to have judicial decisions in many of these cases.

To promote its purposes more aptly, the proposed new procedural law should be drafted in the most general of terms, leaving to each episcopal conference the right to make appropriate applications. Indeed, this is what the same Code Commission is proposing for other sectors of the law, such as that governing Institutes of consecrated life.

### 3. Accountability of Decisions

A third area of concern today in the Church is the fact that, in the case of many administrative actions, a superior is not obliged to account for his decision which is often final, with little actual possibility of recourse.

The establishment of the second section of the Apostolic Signatura in 1967 to resolve 'contentions which have arisen from the exercise of administrative ecclesiastical power and which are referred to it because of an interposed appeal or recourse'[19] has already proven its value and importance for the protection of rights. The decisions of this second section, published on a regular basis, show that in many instances, the rights of the plaintiff were not respected, and the decisions of the authorities were rescinded. Indeed, in a number of cases, even decisions of the offices of the Holy See were reversed.

The possibility of challenging an administrative decision, or of having it reviewed, does not remove a bishop's legislative rights. It simply means that decisions must be taken with greater care, thus providing for greater overall protection of all concerned.

Indeed, the fact that this tribunal exists and is functioning has already made people in authority take cognizance of the procedural norms to be followed, especially when rights are being removed or restricted. There is, however, a slight difficulty. It has now become very difficult for those in office to take quick decisions to settle cases. Offices are sometimes becoming paralyzed by a bureaucratic procedure that was not always required before. With time we will probably find a happy balance between the two extremes.

The study of these three particular points leads us to the realization that we could have a better procedural law that would safeguard the administration of justice and, at the same time, protect the rights of the faithful. In the fourth part of this study we shall consider some changes that could possibly be incorporated into our procedural law to help it meet some of the needs of our times.

### SUGGESTED CHANGES IN PROCEDURAL LAW

Since it seems that the procedural law of the Church, as it now stands, is deficient in some aspects, what suggestions could be made to adapt it even more to the needs of the faithful?

1. The first way would be to find a clear-cut distinction between areas of interest of Church and State, so that the Church's law would be concerned only with the spiritual well-being of the faithful.

2. The law should not be based on the legal system of any particular tradition or region, but should be conducive to the spiritual ends of the Church.

3. The entire judicial process should be set in the context of an enquiry for truth, rather than a settlement of a conflict of rights. The recognition of the truth of a situation is primordial, and any artificial judicial apparatus does not have its place in this context. The courts should not have to be overly concerned with validity or invalidity of individual procedural acts.

4. The law should introduce new presumptions regarding the trustworthiness or credibility of petitioners, or at least remove those that seem to indicate that their word is not to be taken at face value. At a time when people, in most countries, have recourse to the courts of the Church only for peace of conscience, with no civil effects attached to an ecclesiastical decision, we must be able to presume that they are acting in good faith, and, consequently, assign greater juridical value to their depositions.

5. A further point to be mentioned is that greater use of the principle of equity should be foreseen in procedural law. Tribunals should be given greater latitude to take the circumstances of particular cases more into account (for instance, in cases of simulation).

6. Likewise, ecclesiastical judges should be given greater latitude in deciding cases, so that they could base decisions on accepted jurisprudence without having to have continual recourse to an approved canon.

7. The Church could easily recognize the customs of certain countries. It is easy to see that universal rules of law do not always correspond to the mentality of peoples in given areas. For instance, the practices of African customary marriage could be accepted, to a certain degree, to determine according to the 'common estimation of man' the moment when the Church considers the sacrament of matrimony of an indissoluble reality.[20] Procedural law would have to take these important realities into account. The bishops of a territory or region could act collegially to adapt the universal laws to particular situations.

8. Church law in its formulation should leave room for future development. Undoubtedly, we have come a long way thanks to the foresight of the well-organized tribunals, but ecclesial law should not give itself the mission of foreseeing all possibilities.

9. The Church should be open to making a greater use of administrative and of summary procedures in settling cases, rather than proceeding with the detailed formalities of the present—and proposed future—law.

10. One of the most important changes would be to eliminate injustices found in our present legal system. For instance, by permitting judges to forebear signing decisions that in conscience they cannot accept—by allowing for minority opinions. Or, by restricting to parties who would make proper use of them, the acts of a case. Thirdly, by authorizing women to hold positions on tribunals, indeed, in a Church that proclaims the equality of its members, the present discrimination is totally unacceptable. Fourthly, by removing matrimonial cases from an exclusively judicial context so that a plaintiff would have some defense against an uncooperative or deranged respondent who wishes to drag out the proceedings indefinitely. Fifthly, by not obliging the Defender of the Bond to appeal against a decision with which he is in agreement. Other points could be mentioned, but this is an indication of what could be considered under this heading.

## CONCLUSION

This review of post-conciliar legislation has centered on a number of points. We have asked ourselves whether the new law is faithful to the conciliar thrust. In a number of instances, we had to reply in the negative. We saw, though, that in some cases, the organization of the second section of the Apostolic Signature has provided possible relief against arbitrary decisions of ecclesiastical authorities. We also mentioned that the proposed new law on administrative tribunals would provide the faithful with a more accessible means of arbitration and conciliation.

As Pius XII stated, the judicial power is an essential part and a necessary function of the Church.[21] Paul VI, when speaking to the Sacred Roman Rota on January 27, 1969, stated that the pastoral service of the judge must be one of truth, wisdom, justice and Christian prudence.[22] The law will never exist if it prescinds from the spirit of the Gospel, or ignores theological insights, or would stifle the formation of conscience.[23]

The spirit which animates the prudent and wise tribunal must not be a spirit of juridicism, but one 'drawn from the innermost nature of man'.[24]

There still remains a long road to travel to reach the ideal of a law that will be free from secular dominance and more radiant of the gospel of salvation.[25] Much has been done, but we must not lose sight of what remains to be accomplished to provide the people of God with a judicial system that will protect their rights, and at the same time foster their spiritual well-being and progress.

*Notes*

1. Cf. *Gaudium et spes,* no. 86; *Gravissimum Educationis,* nos. 3, 6.
2. Paul VI, Allocution to the Sacred Roman Rota, January 28, 1971, in *A.A.S.* 63 (1971), p. 139. English translation in *The Pope Speaks* 16 (1971-2), p. 76.
3. Paul VI, Allocution to Consociatio Internationalis for the Study of Canon Law, September 17, 1973, in *Origins* 3 (1973-4), p. 272.
4. Motu proprio 'De Episcoporum muneribus', June 15, 1966, in *A.A.S.* 58 (1966), p. 469, no. IV. English translation in *Canon Law Digest* VI, p. 397.
5. Constitution 'Regimini Ecclesiae Universae', August 15, 1967, in *A.S.S.* 59 (1967), p. 921, no. 105.
6. Cf. *Canon Law Digest* VII, pp. 950-66.
7. *A.A.S.* 63 (1971), pp. 480-92.
8. *Ibid.,* p. 482, no. 5. Cf. *Canon Law Digest* VII, p. 915.
9. *A.A.S.* 63 (1971), pp. 441-6.
10. Cf. for instance, the responses of the Commission for Interpretation, *A.A.S.* 65 (1973), p. 620; 66 (1974), p. 462, etc.
11. Cf. *Canon Law Digest* VII, pp. 899-901.
12. Cf. Heinrich Straub, 'De quodam tribunali administrativo in Germania erigendo', in *Periodica* 60 (1971), pp. 591-641.
13 *A.A.S.* 64 (1972), pp. 244-52.
14 *A.A.S.* 65 (1973), pp. 577-81.
15. Not published in *A.A.S.* English text in *Canon Law Digest, Supplement Through 1975,* c. 1962, pp. 1-7.
16. Pontificia Commissio Codici Iuris Canonici Recognoscendo, *Schema canonum de procedura administrativa* (Rome, 1972), 16 pp. Cf. I. Gordon, 'De iustitia administrativa ecclesiastica tum transacto tempore tum hodierno', in *Periodica* 61 (1972), pp. 251-378.
17. *Idem., Schema canonum de modo procedendi pro tutela iurium seu de processibus* (Rome, 1976), xx-97 p.
18. Cf. *A.A.S.* 34 (1942), pp. 338-43, at p. 341. English translation in *Canon Law Digest* III, p. 609.
19. *Loc. cit.,* no. 106. English text in *Canon Law Digest* VI, p. 351.
20. Cf. Pius XII, Allocution to the Sacred Roman Rota, Oct. 1, 1942, in *A.A.S.* 36 (1942), p. 342; cf. *Canon Law Digest* III, p. 610.
21. Cf. Pius XII, Allocution to the Sacred Roman Rota, October 2, 1945, in *A.A.S.* 37 (1945), p. 257, cf. *Canon Law Digest* III, p. 588.
22. Cf. Paul VI, Allocution to the Sacred Roman Rota, January 27, 1969, in *A.A.S.* 61 (1969), p. 176; cf. *Canon Law Digest* VII, p. 903.
23. *Ibid.*
24. *Ibid.,* p. 177; *Canon Law Digest* III, p. 904.
25. Cf. *ibid.*

Enda McDonagh

# The Judgment of Scandal

### THE MORAL THEOLOGY TRADITION

IN the manual tradition of moral theology scandal had a well-defined meaning taken over from Aquinas and with undoubted roots in the New Testament, for example in Mt 18:6ff, Rom 14:15 and 1 Cor 8:9. The tradition persists practically unchanged in more recent and renewed works such as Bernhard Häring's *The Law of Christ* II and Karl Hörmann's *Lexikon der Christlichen Moral.*

The common definition: *factum vel dictum minus rectum praebens (alteri) occasionem ruinae,* envisaged scandal as an external act or word which either because it was wrong in itself or appeared wrong in the circumstances could lead another into sin, his spiritual ruin. The distinctions between direct and indirect dealt with the intention of the scandal-giver; if he intended the sin of the other it was direct; if he merely foresaw and permitted it was indirect. Direct scandal was always wrong but indirect by an action good in itself could be justified in certain circumstances on the criteria of the act of double effect.

This was the background to the Church's pastoral and canonical practice in assessing the damage caused by scandal, forbidding it and punishing it.

Despite its biblical roots and historical respectability this approach to scandal was very inadequate. It did not at all do justice to the full biblical tradition, particularly that of the New Testament. It took little account of the psychological and sociological implications, positive and negative. It belonged to a tradition of moral analysis that was too juridical in form and negative in expression without sufficient attention to the real character of evil in the world. The tradition was too much concerned with individual actions without recognising historical process in which individual actions belonged. And it considered only individual agents and not groups or communities as subjects of moral activity. Any re-appraisal of scandal demands a return to the fuller New Testament concept and its discussion in the larger anthropological context in which theology, including moral theology, works today.

## THE NEW TESTAMENT MESSAGE

It is legitimate here to take for granted the Old Testament linguistic background to the use of *skandalon* and its cognates in the Septuagint and the New Testament. The twofold idea of a trap or snare (originally, a stick setting it off) and obstacle in the way over which one might fall and their transferred religious usage offer an obvious starting-point for the use of the term by Jesus in the Synoptics as well as by Paul and John. And although close linguistic analysis of the kind provided by Stahlin helps a great deal with the New Testament understanding of the term *skandalon*, the reality is richer than the usage of any particular term reveals.

The reality is concerned primarily and predominantly with the strange ways of God with men. That his ways are not conventional human ways is revealed most strikingly and paradoxically in the climactic way of the incarnation, in the Logos made flesh, in the man Jesus who was the Son of God. To complete his historical relationship with men, God adopted not merely human ways, but humanity itself in Jesus the Christ. Yet that foundation stone proved the real stone of stumbling to destruction for his own who were unwilling to receive him (Rom 9:33, 1 Pt 2:6–8). The primary scandal of the New Testament is Jesus himself as Simeon recognised at the outset when he described him as set for the fall and resurrection of many in Israel (Lk 2:34).

In his behaviour and preaching Jesus became increasingly an offence, a scandal to the Jewish people and particularly their religious leaders. His association with sinners, his freedom with the traditions of men, his attitude to the Sabbath and above all his messianic claims proved such a stumbling block that not only was he not accepted in faith as he strove to be but he was rejected, hated and finally put to death. Even some of his own disciples were scandalised at his Eucharistic promises and walked no more with him (Jn 6:61, 66). John the Baptist had his doubts and questions (Mt 11:2–6 par.). The chosen band of faithful with their leader Peter were scandalized at the prospect of his suffering and death (Mt 16:22f) and on its occasion abandoned him in fear and faithlessness (Mk 14:27; Mt 26:31).

The scandal of Jesus provoked the decision of faith or unfaith. Only in faith could he be accepted in his true Messiahship. Those who were unwilling or unable to accept his message, ways and person refused thereby God's saving offer. Instead of faith in Jesus they settled for self-justification through the works of the law (Rom 9:31f). The most loving gift which Yahweh had to offer his own people, his Son, was rejected by so many as the prophets had been before him. The owner of the vineyard could do no more for his people than he had done and they reacted by killing his son (Mk 12:1ff). To the scandal of Jesus' life for his contemporaries was added the scandal of his death. For Paul the scandal of the Cross became the crucial point of faith-decision for Jew and Gentile alike (1 Cor 1:23 etc).

## THE SCANDAL OF GOD'S WAYS WITH MEN

The New Testament data with their Old Testament background take us to the heart of scandal—the scandal of God's ways with men. The saving grace offered above all in Jesus Christ is the *krisis*, the critical point of decision for belief and unbelief. It goes to the heart of human existence itself in final eschatological terms, final fulfilment or final destruction. Scandal is not primarily a question for morality or ethics but a question for faith. Man's ultimate destiny is at stake.

The scandal of Jesus and of the Cross require further and deeper reflexion by theologians and the Church. This New Testament sense has never been entirely lost although it played very little role in moral theology. The belief that the Church or the Christian must never be entirely conformed to this world but must somehow be a sign of contradiction (in Simeon's other term Lk 2:34) has always been recognized, however ambiguously it may have operated in practice. The contradiction or discontinuity can too easily become a self-righteous defensive reaction against the Godgiven signs of the times and lead Church and Christian to rejection of the wider divine call embodied in current history in defence of narrower ecclesiastical interests. The mistakes of the Sadducees and Pharisees are not a first century phenomenon only. Discerning the signs of the times and responding to the divine call beyond its present fixed horizons is a permanent task for Church and Christian. Failure to do so is to be scandalized afresh at the message and power of Jesus. It is a failure in faith, the primary attribute of Christians. The community of the Church as well as the individual Christian may be guilty of this failure and fail to share in the blessing of him who is not scandalized in Jesus (Mt 11:6). Conformity and nonconformity to the sinful world are hereby translated into the call to discern and tread the pilgrim way of faith in hope and love. Undiscerning or blind (Mt 15) self-indulgent and self-protective non-conformity in face of a particular civilization is no more an act of faith than an undiscerning self-indulgent conformity. At the theological and pastoral level the work of listening to and responding to the true call of God as embodied in the world in which we live must continue unremittingly. Mistakes in acceptance and rejection are always possible and as the scandals Jesus predicted, inevitably occur. The challenge of the mistakes is to repentance and a deeper commitment in faith, not to put up the barriers and exclude the world and its God. The more practical applications of this summons to the Church to confront the scandal of his Word in his work will require much fuller consideration.

## THE PARADOX OF LOVE AND EVIL

It is necessary however to pursue more deeply the mystery of the scandal of Jesus Christ and of the Cross. It is part of our accepted wisdom as well as a lesson taught us in so many words in John's first Epistle (1 Jn 4) that to love we must first of all be loved. The more we are loved, the greater capacity we have for love, the more we will love in return. Yet this does not seem to have happened in the case of God's final gift of love, his own Son, the very personification of loving. His love undoubtedly attracted in faith the love of many sinners and ordinary folk. Yet it also provoked hatred and rejection to the point of murder. While he is the paradigm case, Jesus is not alone in human history in this respect. In our own time we have witnessed the assassination of Gandhi and Martin Luther King, the execution of Franz Jägerstätter and Dietrich Bonhoeffer among countless others.

Love at a certain intensity seems to intensify and reveal the deeper evil in man. It is as if, to adapt Eliot's words, we can bear only a little loving. More systematically it means that we have to take more seriously the forces of evil in the world and the fact that the intensification of loving in a particular individual or community provokes its counterpart in the intensification of evil or hatred. Perhaps this is part of the background to the exorcism stories in the New Testament as it certainly seems to be part of the divisiveness which Jesus introduced into the world 'bringing not peace but the sword' and setting father against son, mother against daughter (Mt 10:34 par.). It would also throw light on the evil which the followers of Gandhi and Martin Luther King called forth from the servants of the establishment which they opposed.

In endeavoring to understand the New Testament meaning of scandal as a test or crisis point we have to pay more attention to the evil which is structured into our world. Traditional moral theology tended to analyse scandal and human behaviour in general without sufficient awareness of this evil and of the ambiguity which it creates in all of us,

Christian and nonChristian, Church and world. Given such an awareness it is more necessary to follow the path of Jesus Christ in faith and
hope irrespective of the scandal it causes and the evil it provokes. But
it is salutary to recall that the ambiguity also affects Church and Christian and that the evil inherent in them may in their reaction to genuine
love and prophetic action be intensified to the point of rejecting a
further manifestation of Jesus within or without the confines of the
visible Church.

The further reaches of the mystery of the scandal of Jesus extend to
the favourite Pauline presentation of it in terms of the scandal of the
Cross. The elimination of Jesus the blasphemous scandalizer on
the Cross seemed to guarantee the triumph of hatred over love to the
believing and the just execution of a disturber and criminal to the
unbelieving. Both were confounded in the Resurrection. When hatred
had done its worst, reached its peak and removed the scandalous
threat, it had in fact undermined itself. The love even unto dying
triumphed over dying in the Resurrection. The worst that hatred could
achieve proved the gateway to the ultimate triumph of love. The believers were confounded in their brief infidelity and restored in their faith.
To the unbelievers the very criminal execution itself could only seem
scandalous and foolish as a basis for the preaching of God's achievement of salvation and reconciliation. The scandal of his death was all
the more potent for those who had never known him in life. Paul's
insistence on the scandal of it as the paradoxical giving of new life to all
men by God revealed the crisis point for faith in God's ways transcending any self-domination or self-justification by man. The test of fidelity
to this achievement must be the embodiment of the scandal of the
Cross in Christian living with all the risks that entails for misunderstanding, derision and rejection.

### WARNING AGAINST SCANDAL

A further aspect of the puzzling scandal of Jesus Christ was his
concern to avoid scandal in paying the temple tax, for example (Mt
17:27). His condemnation of those through whom scandals would
come, inevitable though they be, was developed in his admonition to
sacrifice eye or limb should it be an occasion of scandal (Mt 18 par). He
was not a deliberate provoker of the scandal which concerned him, the
lapsing from faith into final destruction. This teaching, together with
Paul's concern in his letters to the Romans (14:15) and Corinthians (1
Cor 8:9) about sacrificing one's freedom to avoid actions that might be
the occasion of another's lapse, provided the background to the moral

theological tradition. However, it was divorced in this tradition both from the scandal of Jesus himself, from an awareness of the wider evil, and impoverished by its neglect of the eschatological faith risk which informed the treatment by Jesus and Paul.

## PASTORAL IMPLICATIONS

It is time to draw some tentative pastoral conclusions from this attempt to re-establish a true theological basis for the understanding and judgment of scandal.

The Church itself, in word and more particularly in deed, in its life and structures, must manifest to all men the scandal of Jesus Christ as a call to faith. It will seek to do this in a manner calculated to draw men to Christ by attending to the genuine signs and characteristics of Jesus which the particular civilization embodies. And it must do so, conscious of the risk of intensification of evil and rejection which this may entail. Its identification with the poor and neglected rather than a courting of the rich and powerful is a useful criterion in assessing the true scandal of the Church. Its own structures and activities as a community dedicated to truth, freedom and justice for all its members and ultimately for mankind will prevent the scandal of human weakness from obscuring the scandal of divine love. In the prevention of participation by so many members in Church life, in the inadequacy of structures for communication and judgment, in the preference for power rather than truth or justice, in the need for a new life-style for clergy, religious and laity, the scandal of man's ways in the Church is frequently manifested. The indefectibility of the Church based on the divine promise should not make it complacent about the urgent call of continually displacing the scandal of human weakness to reveal the true scandal of Jesus Christ.

## RESPONSE TO SCANDAL

However, the scandal of human weakness will always be part of the Church as a whole. The ambiguity of human endeavour always presupposes the fearful reality of evil at the heart of our best endeavour. So the Church has to provide room for creative experiment and prophetic word and action that may to human weakness appear scandalous in the primary Christian sense. Its response to such experiment and prophecy must be one of faith, seeking to understand and discriminate between the gracious God-given and the sinful man-laden. It must be one of patience because, Gamaliel-fashion, the Church should let the community through time arrive at a considered judgment. It must be one of love because the experimenter and the prophet need the loving support of the community if they are not to be isolated socially and psychologically and be distorted in their rôle into cranks and eccentrics.

Assessment in faith and response in love are not easy and may not always seem adequate to the truth of Christ or the life of the community. The temptation to turn them into a juridical sentence with or without a due process may be irresistible. Such a process and sentence may indeed be sometimes demanded but it should be on the very rare occasion when faith and love have seemed to fail utterly in keeping the agent in genuine communication with the community of the Church. And such process must be directed to restoring that communication as quickly as possible. For the process to achieve this the community as a whole must share in it in a representative capacity and one-man or arbitrary exercises of authority only compound the scandal.

Where the human weakness has no creative pretentions the faith and love response remains primary. How far such human weakness constitutes scandal depends very much on the actual person involved, his circumstances and those of the possibly scandalized as well as their capacity to discriminate in faith and love in response. And this is the lead that should first of all be given to them. Again the judicial procedure is a last resort but must bear all the marks of fairness in seeking a reconciliation in faith and love.

The traditional moral theological treatment of scandal with its canonical counterpart clearly does not reflect the thrust of the New Testament teaching. It ignores the true challenge of scandal in theological terms as a summons to faith and love. It does not provide for truly creative Christian experiments or genuine prophetic voices and the difficulties in assessing these. In areas as diverse as doctrinal development, the life-style of religious communities or priests, prayer movements, liberation movements, inter-Church worship and communion, inter-Church marriages, inter-Church schooling, and the pastoral and sacramental care of the divorced and homosexual, room for growth through experimentation must be maintained against any self-righteous cries of 'scandal'.

In responding to the scandal of human weakness the same faith in discrimination and love in support is required of the individual Christian and the Christian community. This is more likely to ensure the maturity in Christ to which all Christians are summoned than easy recourse to moral and canonical condemnations, necessary though these may be as a very last resort.

*Bibliography*

St Alphonsus, *Theologia Moralis,* I, II.
L. Baas—P. Brand, 'Über das Ärgernis,' *Gott in Welt,* II (Freiburg, 1964).
B. Häring, *The Law of Christ,* II (1962).
K. Hörmann, *Lexikon der Christlichen Moral* (Munich, 1969).
N. Jung, 'Scandale', *Dict. de Theol. Cath.* XIV (Paris, 1939).
X. Léon-DuFour, *Vocabulaire de théologie biblique* (Paris, 1962).
P. G. Michiels, *De Delictis* (Lublin, 1934).
W. Molinski, 'Scandal,' *Sacramentum Mundi* VI (London, 1970).
A. Nolden—A. Schmitt, *Summa Theologiae Moralis* (Barcelona, 1951).
Stählin, G., *Theological Dictionary of the New Testament,* VII (1971).
B. Stoeckle, 'Ärgernis', *Wörterbuch Christlicher Ethik* (Freiburg, 1975).
St Thomas Aquinas, *Sum. Theol. II.*

John Noonan

# Public Judgment in the Church

ON June 30, 1924, by a judgment of the Apostolic Signatura, the marriage of Filippo Folchi-Vici to Pauline Bailly, contracted in April 1891, was definitely declared to be null. Filippo had left Pauline for another girl in 1896 and opened his suit for an annulment in 1906. In 1908, the court of the Vicariate of Rome held his marriage good; within the year this decision was affirmed by the Sacred Congregation of the Council. By special rescripts of Pius X, the case was referred back to this congregation and then to the Sacred Roman Rota, which, in 1909, again affirmed the validity of the marriage. On appeal in 1910, the Apostolic Signatura sent the case back for rehearing by the Rota. In 1912 the Rota held the marriage good. In 1922, by special rescript of Pius XI, the case was re-opened in the Rota; and in 1923 the Rota held the marriage non-existent. It was this decision which was affirmed by the Signatura in 1924, thereby ending Folchi's marriage irrevocably thirty-three years after it had been solemnized in Rome. The basis for the decision was that, in 1891, Filippo, who already had two sons by Pauline and who became the father of seven other children by other women, had determined within his mind to exclude further offspring from her.[1]

When the Folchi case is first read, it looks as though it might be a fluke or anomaly. But its principal characteristics are those of most current matrimonial litigation: the outcome depends on the reading of the recesses of the human heart; this reading of such a subjective region is itself highly subjective, so judges will vary in their perception; procedural favours from the Pope can affect the outcome, particularly because repeated hearings will increase the likelihood of a defect being discovered; mercy will incline Pope and judges to discover a defect.[2] It is unlikely that any student of jurisprudence would think that the Folchi case's eighteen years and six decisions and two papal interventions illustrated the ideal of public judgment. Yet, if I am correct about its salient characteristics, some or all of them are present in most of the marriage cases in the modern courts of the Church. What will be discovered to have been the internal intent and psychological condition of the participants will depend on the skill of counsel who collect and present the facts and on the percipience of the judges who hear them. Papal favour can affect procedure. Mercy is a weight toward finding invalidity. In these circumstances it is not strange that there is great variety among dioceses in the number of annulments granted; that there is great variety among auditors of the Rota in perceiving nullity; and that the value of public judgments in this area is not evident.

Could the characteristics of the system be changed in order to give public judgment a useful function? Most obviously to those bred on Montesquieu, a greater separation of powers could be effected, so that the Pope would surrender his procedural control over the Rota. As he has already delegated his decisional authority to this body, no theoretical objection would exist to this further divestiture. The Rota could be made a truly independent court. It is also clear that a return could be made to the jurisprudence in effect before 1900.[3] Internal intention and psychological state could be disregarded. Strict justice could be insisted upon, and mercy eliminated as an element in the exercise of judicial discretion. Would we want this kind of system for judging marriages within the Church?

The first reaction of a Catholic to the story of Filippo Folchi's annulment is apt to be envy: he had the right connections at the Curia, so he got what he wanted. But does not the envy point to a truth: we want the decision of these matters to be made by a merciful friend. No one would be envious if every suppliant received the royal treatment accorded Folchi. Why should not everyone have it? Why should it be available only by access to the Curia?

As long as the Church took on the task of the upholding of the social fabric, its judgments on marriage affected property and the custody of children. In most of the world the Church no longer has the task, and its judgments no longer have those effects. The emphasis on internal intention and psychological state has come with this change in mission.[4] Christian marriage has become primarily a religious commitment. Do we really want to treat it as though we were deciding property rights? The nature of the matter, joined with our expectations of the Church, may lead us to conclude not that public judgment should be perfected, but that it should be eliminated. If the Church is to deal with intention and psychological state on matters where mercy is as important as justice, it is the private judgment of penitent and of confessor, not the public judgment of a tribunal, which is called for. The Rota and the diocesan courts are vestiges which the time has come to eliminate.

To such a sweeping purification of the process, two objections may be raised. First, marriage is an agreement between two persons according them certain rights. To decide that such an agreement is invalid is to deny the existence of these rights. So to decide is an act of justice. Whether these rights exist or not must be justly ascertained. To investigate them secretly with only one party present in the manner of the confessional would be unjust. Secondly, although the Church no longer sustains the social order in most of the world, marriage within the Christian community is a social institution. It is a sign and therefore inescapably exists as a social form. It is a sign of the union of Christ and the Church and, *a fortiori*, its existence or non-existence is of significance to the ecclesiastical community. It cannot be terminated in a private fashion.

The first of these replies is countered by a prevailing practice. For over fifty years the Popes have dissolved marriages 'in favour of the faith'. These dissolutions have been categorized as administrative, not judicial acts. They have been conventionally analyzed and presented as acts of grace, given to a petitioner. No hearing is granted the other party to the union. In many cases that party does not know of the proceeding. In at least some cases—*Djakarta, August 19, 1959* is illustrative—one of the parties whose marriage the Pope dissolved may not have even known of the existence of the Pope. Unless this established practice of Pius XI, Pius XII, John XXIII, and Paul VI is to be pronounced unjust, a marriage may be ended as far as the Church is concerned without a trial.[5]

The second reply points to a more serious problem. Since at least A.D. 410 the Church has publicly decided marriage cases. If the bilateral contractual aspects of marriage do not require a tribunal, perhaps its social aspects do. As a sign of unity, however, marriage communicates only if there is a live affection between the spouses. If that is dead, the marriage may still be valid and indissoluble, but the function of the marriage as sign of Christ and the Church has been frustrated. Who would say that Pauline Bailly in Milan and Filippo Folchi living with another woman in Rome communicated to anyone by their marriage a sense of the love of Christ for the Church? The theological conclusion that Christian marriage is a sign of that love cannot be a substitute for observation of what happens when two persons have separated and each loathes the other. A sign which no longer speaks is no longer a sign in society, secular or Christian.

Litigated marriage cases today are virtually always unions like the Folchis' where the couple is hopelessly divided and there is no likelihood of reconciliation. In countries which permit civil divorce the spouses are usually divorced. Quite often they are civilly remarried to others or living in concubinage with others. Although their Christian marriage may be indissoluble, it does not function as a social sign. There can scarcely be a social requirement that its validity should be determined by a public judgment.

I conclude that there are no strong reasons today for the existence of tribunals to try and publicly pronounce on marriage cases; that the present practice is a hybrid mixing elements appropriate to a penitential system with the system of justice; and that the vestigial forms of public judgment should be eliminated. There is no theological requirement that they should exist.

Up to this point this paper has looked at the most common type of judgment in the contemporary Church. At one time marriage represented less than five percent of the judicial business of the courts of the Curia. Their work was once largely concerned with controversies between ecclesiastics over benefices, jurisdictional boundaries, privileges, and the like. In the course of the eighteenth century most of these matters came to be handled administratively.[6] They are essentially matters of institutional management or housekeeping. Again, it is difficult to perceive any theological reason to return to the judicial mode.[7]

The judicial mode, imperfect as was its use, was also eventually abandoned by the Sacred Congregation of the Inquisition and its successor congregations. In part, no doubt, the absence of any secular penalty for heresy meant that the trial of a person for heresy no longer had the lugubrious drama and dreadful possibilities it once held. In part, modern notions of fair process made the old methods of trial unsupportable. But fair trials with only ecclesiastical penalties as sanction could be held. If the judicial model is not now used to examine heresy, it must be because of a general recognition that a person is larger than his doctrine; that it is consequently a mistake to try the person when it is his doctrine you seek to isolate and reject; and that the appropriate object for examination is not a given human being but a particular tenet or set of tenets. Contemporary theology, in its distinction between erroneous doctrine and the person, supports this insight.

For the examination of teaching, a judicial forum is inappropriate. What is needed is not the clash of advocates operating within the narrow framework of a set of issues, but informed discussion by competent persons. The best way to a wise decision, writes an experienced advocate, is that of 'a few candid people pooling their minds on a problem, and not so much arguing with each other as eliciting each other's arguments'.[8] Judicial trial is a poor second best. For teaching doctrine we should take the best way.

But, it may be objected, we are not merely seeking a wise result. The best way is the way of sages and scholars, but we are not dealing with pure scholarship. When a conclusion as to heresy or error is reached, it will be promulgated by the Sacred Congregation for the Teaching of the Faith or by the Pope himself. It will have extrinsic authority from this promulgation. If the conclusion is that certain doctrine is inconsistent with the premises of the Christian faith, the reputation of the teachers of that doctrine will be injured.

That injury, I venture to suppose, will not be substantial today, unless the opinion promulgated by authority is persuasive on its merits. If the asserted inconsistency is shown, if the errors criticized are established, if the arguments in favor of them are refuted, the teacher's reputation will be injured, as it would be hurt if his work was subjected to damaging criticism by his peers. The risk of criticism is the scholar's risk. The risk of criticism by ecclesiastical authority does not materially enlarge the theological scholar's exposure.

Suppose, however, that consequences follow for the teacher whose doctrine is criticized as unChristian. Suppose that he is subject to removal from his position at a Catholic university because he is teaching heresy. Even in the year 1977 such a possibility cannot be categorically excluded. In such a case natural justice requires that the teacher should have a hearing and that he should be permitted to show that his doctrine has been misunderstood, and that it is not unChristian.

Such a hearing would be within the institution where he teaches; its intramural character would keep it from being public in a juridical sense; yet, almost inevitably, it would turn into a junior, or academic, heresy trial, in which the teacher as a person would be on trial with his teaching. The notion is repugnant. It would be to continue, in an academic forum, a type of process which has become obsolete as a form of ecclesiastical discipline. If heresy trials conducted by the Inquisition are offensive to the person, they are equally offensive if conducted by a university committee. The accountability of teachers is to their peers in the ordinary mode of scholarly review and criticism. It would be wrong to provide judicial safeguards for the accused teacher because it would be wrong to try him in the first place.

The corollary of this conclusion, of course, is that teachers cannot be removed on charges of heresy and that university theological faculties must be prepared to tolerate the range of explicit belief now typical of a number of Anglican institutions.[9] Given the extraordinary balance needed to teach orthodox theology and the likelihood of the most explicitly orthodox teacher cherishing implicit heresy, it is problematic whether such tolerance will increase the actual amount of unorthodox doctrine taught.[10] It is certain that such tolerance is necessary if theology is to be practised as an academic profession.

There remains the wide area of activity which is not academic but pastoral and where the Church acts visibly by bishops, priests, religious, and laity. There are those, perhaps, who would defend a tolerance of opinions and lifestyles in pastoral activity too, insensibly adapting the Church to the pluralism characteristic of Western secular society. But preaching a constant doctrine and living within certain boundaries constitute the Church as a community. Let us suppose, on the one hand, a bishop who teaches that the second Vatican Council was without authority and a priest who teaches that only those who profess obedience to the Pope can be saved. Let us suppose, on the other hand, a bishop who ordains self-proclaimed, active homosexuals, and let us suppose a religious superior of women who sponsors an abortion clinic. Let us also suppose a pastor, without special ideological commitments, who is an habitual drunkard. As the Church is a community, such persons must be prevented from harming other members of the community in their discharge of their community responsibilities. They must be suspended or removed from office. Justice requires that such discipline should be administered with due process for the accused: charges clearly formulated, an opportunity to deny them, and a hearing before someone other than the accuser. Unless waived by the accused, public judgment is called for.

No doubt there will be those who would turn such processes into heresy trials for the sake of the defendant and in order to advance a particular point of view. They mistake their forum. If ideas cannot win acceptance in the theological arena, they should not be put forward for vindication in a judicial proceeding. In other words, the conclusion that heresy trials are a poor way to the truth should be adhered to; the notion of trying a person as a person is to be resisted. When a minister of the Church is charged with violating the rules of the Church by his public teaching or conduct, judgment must be not of his person, but of his act.

Is such judgment, however, compatible with the demands of love? In focusing on the act the judge objectifies it and isolates it from the person who performed it. He responds to the act and not the man. If the judge took into account all the factors of personality, if he entered empathetically into the spirit of the accused, he would understand the bizarre behaviour, not condemn the actor. But judgment inevitably moves from condemnation of the act to the imposition of a penalty on the person whose act is judged. To say that the penalty is medicinal appears often to be heartless sophistry: if medicinal, why is it not prescribed by a psychiatrist who knows the patient? The person guilty of the condemned act appears to be punished for the benefit of the community: so treated, he is treated like a thing.[11] Does not the judge, then, violate his Christian duty to love him as himself?

The judge, however, has an obligation to love other members of the community, too. If one member is harming them, love of that person cannot take precedence over love of the others. The judge in exercise of his love of the others must prevent an abusive minister from doing this harm. Justice, in Augustine's sublime definition, is 'love serving the one loved';[12] the one loved must include these others. To the extent that he prevents harm to them, it would be foolish to characterize his behaviour as loveless. Removal from office is an essential sanction of the community. But excommunication, removal from the community as a whole, is a sanction which rarely if ever could be justified as necessary.

In the past the ecclesiastical judge of a sinful act was often seen as vindicating the honour of God. By a process familiar to historians of religion, notions of secular conduct were projected on to God, and the idea of God so formed was then used as a divine model for human imitation.[13] St Anselm visualized God avenging affronts to his honour.[14] The instances of ecclesiastical judges avenging divine honor which have been preserved in Gratian could not be understood by anyone today as acts of love.[15]

'Swear not at all' (Mt 5:34). 'Lend freely, hoping nothing thereby' (Lk 6:35). 'Judge not lest you be judged' (Mt 7:1). None of these pithy exhortations attributed to Jesus have been taken literally by the Church. Yet, unless they are to be ignored, they must give direction to community conduct. Public judgment is to be kept to a minimum—to what is necessary to remove from their function those who abuse it.

This conclusion is powerfully reinforced by the daily prayer of the Church which, in some form, comes from Jesus himself. The Christian community is hardly exempt from the obligation to forgive as it wants the Father to forgive. In such a community, public judgment has a small, subsidiary function.

## Notes

1. For a detailed history of the case, see John T. Noonan, Jr., *Power to Dissolve: Lawyers and Marriages in the Courts of the Roman Curia* (Cambridge, Mass., 1962), pp. 159–238.

2. *Ibid.*, pp. 394–402.

3. *Ibid.*, p. 192.

4. *Ibid.*, pp. 218–9.

5. *Ibid.*, pp. 366–90.

6. *Ibid.*, pp. 182–3.

7. The kind of review by the Signatura, provided for in Paul VI, *Regimini Ecclesiae, A.A.S. 59* (1967), p. 921, may be assimilated to the judgments in disciplinary cases discussed below.

8. Charles Curtis, *It's Your Law* (Boston, 1949), p. 5.

9. Whether seminary teaching should be considered an academic or pastoral activity for these purposes depends on what level of teaching and research is expected of the seminary.

10. Karl Rahner, 'On Heresy', *Inquiries,* trans. W. J. O'Hara (New York, 1964), p. 444.

11. Cf. Oliver Wendell Holmes, Jr., *The Common Law* (Boston, 1881), p. 44, referring to the objection that the criminal law treats a man as a thing: 'If a man lives in society, he is liable to find himself so treated'.

12. Augustine, *De moribus ecclesiae catholicae et de moribus Manichaeorum* 1.15, 125, *Patrologia latina,* ed. J. P. Migne, 32, p. 132.

13. See Mircea Eliade, *The Myth of the Eternal Return,* W. R. Trask trans. (New York, 1954), pp. 23–4; *Idem, Mephistopheles and the Androgyne: Studies in Religious Myth and Symbol,* trans. J. M. Cohen (New York, 1965), pp. 206–7.

14. Anselm, *Cur Deus Homo* 1, 13, *PL* 158, pp. 378–9.

15. See, e.g., Gratian, *Decretum,* ed. E. Friedberg, *Corpus iuris canonici* I (Leipzig, 1879–1881), C.27 q.1 c.18–9 (Pope Gregory the Great prescribing the punishment of a nun who left her cloister).

Joseph Byron

# The Case of the Washington Nineteen:
# A Search for Justice

IN accepting the invitation to write the present article I had in mind to attempt to distance myself from the events of which I speak by always writing in the third person. However, I find that simply too artificial and awkward. Since I was a part of these events, this article cannot help being something of a personal chronicle; and I see no point in trying to translate it into an abstraction.

'The Case of the Washington Nineteen' is the name popularly given to the canonical process on behalf of a group of priests in Washington, D.C. who had been penalized by their bishop, Cardinal Patrick A. O'Boyle. (Actually, the canonical side began long before any of the priests attempted to enter a formal case, but we did not know it at the time.)

The experience I speak of began at about the time of the issuing of the encyclical *Humane vitae* on July 29, 1968. Many responses to that document were printed in time, but among the first was a statement by a group of theologians, largely North Americans. Upon publication of the theologians' statement a group of Washington priests publicly issued a 'Statement of Conscience' which expressed in general terms the pastoral approach they intended to take with people who were caught in the birth control dilemma.

I do not intend to go into the content of the Statement of Conscience or of the 'pastoral solution' which was achieved almost three years later under the aegis of the Vatican's Sacred Congregation for the Clergy, and is embodied in a series of 'Findings' issued by the Congregation. I speak only of the experience and the process which were initiated by the former document and terminated by the latter. The documents themselves are matters of public record.

Shortly after the publication of the priests' Statement of Conscience, Cardinal O'Boyle communicated with each priest individually, requiring that each make an individual retraction of the statement. This began a protracted period of discussions with the Cardinal. The discussions took place mainly in a series of meetings called by Cardinal O'Boyle at which he met each of the priests individually. The subject matter of these meetings had to do mostly with the Statement of Conscience, its meaning, interpretation, and implications, and the need to repudiate it.

In these meetings the Cardinal was flanked by advisers and a notary; the priest being questioned was always alone. We were never represented by counsel; nor did there seem to be any need for it in the beginning, since it was not apparent that we were involved in a canonical procedure. At some point, however, it became a canonical procedure. I am not exactly sure when this happened, since we were never informed. When we began to suspect that there were canonical implications in what was happening, we did attempt to bring a canon lawyer with us to one of the meetings with the Cardinal. As soon as his presence was recognized, the Cardinal dismissed him with the statement: 'We don't need you, Father. I have a canon lawyer'.

During this same period, on more than one occasion, the Cardinal sought from us something in writing which would clarify or temper the position we had taken and would in fact be a retraction of it.

Apparently, during this period canonical procedures were being observed prior to the imposition of penalties, although we did not know it. Later, when the case reached Rome, and we did have the advice of counsel, the canonists representing us were permitted to read the minutes of these proceedings; and they had to admit that all the canonical norms had been complied with.

Eventually, on September 30, 1968, canonical penalties were imposed, varying in severity from one individual to another, apparently on the basis of the answers given to certain specific questions, both orally and in writing.

For some time before the imposition of penalties, the priests were convinced that the meetings between us and Cardinal O'Boyle were making no progress toward a resolution of the dispute. We therefore focused our efforts on trying to obtain the assistance of mutually acceptable third parties in the role of conciliator or mediator. In particular we would have welcomed the assistance of the already existing Committee on Arbitration and Mediation of the National Conference of Catholic Bishops of the United States. However, the assistance of such a mediating element could only occur if it were acceptable to both parties, and Cardinal O'Boyle did not find any such intervention acceptable. Nevertheless, even after the penalties were imposed efforts toward securing the services of such third parties continued to be made by the priests, but without success.

This attempt at mediation was the first effort to introduce a measure of 'due process' into a situation in which the Bishop was prosecutor, judge, jury, and enforcer of penalties once they had been decreed. It was the first step in the 'search for justice' which I will attempt to chronicle in the present article. Admittedly these first attempts sought to by-pass a formal judicial process in the hope of finding some less cumbersome avenue to impartiality. However, we always knew that if the informal procedures remained unavailable, the right to a formal judicial trial was available to every member of the Church. We were labouring under a misapprehension, as subsequent events were to prove.

In Spring 1969 initial steps were taken toward seeking a formal judicial trial, it having been determined that everything else had been tried, and this was the only route left open. Admittedly, church law does provide for the possibility of direct recourse to the competent Roman Congregation, but we were most apprehensive about becoming involved in another administrative process, as secretive as the one to which we had already been subject, and with none of the guarantees which we considered essential to a fair and impartial hearing. Not all the penalized priests were interested in submitting themselves to the Church's judicial system. However, nineteen priests out of forty who had been penalized chose to take the judicial route–somewhat reluctantly–simply because they felt that they had no other choice. The canonical expertise would be supplied by a volunteer Committee of Concerned Canon Lawyers, with the sponsorship and support of the National Federation of Priests' Councils.

The case was first entered in the court of the Archdiocese of Washington in September of 1969, in the name of Reverend Joseph Byron *et alii* (the other eighteen priests). We were at pains to avoid giving cause for thinking that we were attempting to name Cardinal O'Boyle as defendant in the case and were quite willing to be the defendants ourselves. Nevertheless, the court judged that Cardinal O'Boyle was in fact being cast in the rôle of defendant, and for this reason declared itself incompetent, since only the Holy Father is competent to judge a Cardinal.

A further attempt was made to have the case accepted by the tribunal of the Diocese of Cleveland, the designated Court of Appeal for the Archdiocese of Washington. However, the Cleveland Court concurred with that of Washington in the belief that Cardinal O'Boyle was in fact, if not in name, being cast in the rôle of defendant in the case. Therefore they declared themselves incompetent to judge it, since only the Holy Father is competent to judge a Cardinal.

At this point the Committee of Concerned Canon Lawyers advised that there was really no point in trying to carry the judicial process any further, for an appeal to the Sacred Roman Rota would surely produce only the same results. Their conclusion was that we had now proven conclusively that there was no judicial recourse available to the priests; for an appeal to the Pope would remove the matter from the judicial sphere and allow for only a purely administrative judgment.

Nevertheless, the nineteen priests unanimously agreed to continue with the one procedure left open to them and make their appeal directly to the Holy Father. The Committee of Canon Lawyers for their part argeed to continue to assist. Thereupon, an appeal was sent to the Pope which asked, in essence, that the penalties levelled against the nineteen priests be reviewed in terms of whether they really were justified by the facts of the case. The petition specifically requested that his Holiness establish a quasi-judicial procedure by allowing the appeal to be dealt with by some competent body in which there would be an opportunity for open review of the evidence, rebuttal of charges, and such other characteristics as are considered to be essential to the fair and impartial administration of justice.

This appeal was directed to the Holy Father on February 11, 1970. On April 18, 1970, a letter was directed to me by the Apostolic Delegate to the United States in which he stated that the letter which I had sent to the Holy Father on behalf of myself and the other eighteen priests had been received and that a reply would soon be forthcoming.

The reply when it came was in the form of a letter dated April 10, 1970, from the Vatican Secretary of State, Cardinal Villot. In his own name and in the name of the Holy Father the Cardinal urged the nineteen priests to re-open conversations with their Bishop in a spirit of charity and mutual trust. This would surely lead to an amicable solution which would preclude the need for any further canonical procedures.

The priests received this reply with great dismay, since such conversations had been conducted before at considerable length but with no results except canonical penalties for us. It was precisely from such a fate that we had asked to be delivered.

However, there was one ray of hope. The Holy Father did not stipulate anything concerning the manner in which such conversations should take place. As a matter of fact the tone of the letter from his Secretary of State and of a covering letter from the Apostolic Delegate, Archbishop Raimondi, left open the possibility that the process could be a true 'conciliation' brought about by a neutral third party or parties. The Apostolic Delegate in his letter to me spoke of a 'new effort . . . consistent with the accepted principle of a preliminary conciliatory approach.' In closing, he further stated: 'Should any clarification be desired, I will be glad to offer my assistance'.

Our canon lawyers and I wanted to know if the term 'preliminary conciliatory approach' could be understood in the sense in which conciliation is defined in *A Summary of Actions Taken by the National Conference of Catholic Bishops on the Subject of Due Process*, pp. 13–5 ('Process for Conciliation'): 'Unmediated dialogue becomes debate; each participant, therefore, must have the opportunity of stating his side of the conflict to a conciliator who will attempt to lead the participants to be reconciled with one another'. We knew that the Holy Father's message did not rule out such a process of conciliation. What we hoped for was some measure of positive support for it, since this is what we had been seeking all along.

Therefore, it was decided that I should attempt to avail myself of the offer of assistance by the Apostolic Delegate, and seek support at least for this small measure of due process. With the thought of asking him whether 'conciliatory' could be understood in the sense in which it is defined above I asked for an interview with Archbishop Raimondi. He replied that I should put my question in writing. I put it in writing, and the Delegate replied: 'It seems to me that the answer to your inquiry may be found in the letter of Cardinal Villot'.

There would be no help from that quarter.

However, there remained the possibility that Cardinal O'Boyle would himself consent to a true process of conciliation according to the standards established by the American bishops, since nothing precluded such a course. Accordingly, we approached Cardinal O'Boyle with a request that the new conversations should take place in the form of such a process of conciliation. However, Cardinal O'Boyle took the position that such a course would not be in keeping with the exhortation of Cardinal Villot, and/or such a process could only be undertaken by authorization of the Holy See.

During the Spring of 1970 there followed a considerable amount of correspondence involving Cardinal O'Boyle, Cardinal Villot, Archbishop Raimondi, and myself on behalf of the nineteen priests. The theme rarely varied. For our part, we repeatedly renewed our request for due process of some kind, focusing in particular on a request for conciliation–admittedly the most innocuous and watered-down form of due process, but the only one we had any realistic hope of getting at the time. On the part of the prelates with whom we were corresponding the reply was always a variation on the theme that we were not being denied due process, had never been denied due process, canonical or otherwise, but we should seek to settle the dispute through amiable and amicable conversation with our bishop.

By mid-Summer both we and our canonical advisers had just about concluded that this impasse would never be broken, when unexpectedly there arrived a letter from Cardinal Villot in which it was stated that our case had been turned over to the competent Sacred Congregation for the Clergy for examination and decision. At the time of the receipt of the letter we did not really understand what this new action might mean; but it was in fact the granting of our often repeated request for the involvement of a neutral and competent third party in the settlement of the case.

With the sending of the case to the Congregation for the Clergy it became largely the responsibility of Cardinal John Wright, the Prefect of that Congregation, who throughout the remainder of the process demonstrated a sincere desire to provide the fair and impartial hearing for which we had been asking, as well as great generosity with his time and personal interest.

Since there was no precedent for the handling of the case, Cardinal Wright devised a procedure in three stages. In phase one there would be a sifting and evaluation of the material submitted to the Congregation—by impartial persons outside the Congregation—in order to produce a series of specific questions for discussion. In phase two proxies for Cardinal O'Boyle and proxies for the nineteen priests would meet in Rome with members of the Congregation, one of whom would act as chairman for the discussions. In this phase it was hoped that those representing the principals would reach some measure of agreement, though perhaps not total agreement. In phase three the parties to the previous phase would present to the Cardinal-prefect those things they might wish to submit to him for final resolution. The Congregation itself with the Cardinal as Prefect would make a final evaluation and issue its findings as the basis upon which a solution to the long-standing conflict might be achieved.

I agreed to this process in the name of all nineteen priests and Cardinal O'Boyle accepted it. We each named our proxies for the Cardinal, Msgr. E. Robert Arthur and Rev. John Donoghue; for the priests, Rev. Raymond Goedert and Rev. Donald Heintschel.

Cardinal Wright quickly named the participants of phase one of the process and their work was soon accomplished. This brings us to late January/early February, 1971. The second phase began in late February and lasted for approximately two weeks. I was able to be in Rome personally during that time. Since the nature of the case, and the process agreed to, demanded that the deliberations be conducted by the proxies, it was not possible for me to be present along with Father Goedert and Father Heintschel at the official sessions. However, I did have the opportunity to review the progress of the discussions with them after each meeting, and from my point of view this was a crucial ingredient for the success of the process.

Phase two was completed and the proxies and I returned home by the end of the second week of March, 1971. Towards the end of April word was received that the Congregation for the Clergy had met to evaluate the work accomplished in phase two and a set of 'findings' would be forthcoming.

The findings were delivered to me personally in the presence of Fathers Heintschel and Goedert by Monsignor Albert Bovone, Head of the Priests' Section of the Congregation for the Clergy. The date was April 29, 1971. As I mentioned previously these findings are a matter of public record; and I am not discussing their content, but only the process. It was very simple at this point. Any priest who had incurred a suspension could go to Cardinal O'Boyle, say that he accepted the findings of the Congregation, and ask to have his faculties restored. Such requests were granted without further question. No other statement was required, either orally or in writing.

Within the course of the next few weeks, most of the nineteen priests who had submitted their case to the canonical process sought, and were granted, a restoration of faculties by Cardinal O'Boyle, the others having meanwhile left the active ministry or the archdiocese. The 'Washington Case' was terminated, approximately two years and nine months after the issuing of the original statement of conscience. Of the forty priests who had originally experienced some suspension of faculties less than half were still engaged in the active ministry.

Cardinal Wright has been justly praised for the very real pastoral concern which he brought to the solution of this case once it reached his Congregation. It has also been said that the process he devised for dealing with the case was an ingenious solution and probably the only one which would have worked under the circumstances.

These accolades are truly deserved; and it represents no denial of them to note, nevertheless, that by the time the case reached Cardinal Wright it was bound up in a set of circumstances which put the Cardinal under some constraints regarding the kind of process we could use.

Since by that time it was absolutely certain that no process would work if the principals were involved—that it had to be done through proxies–some of the openness of a normal judicial process had to be forsworn. For instance, I do not know to this day what exactly was the nature of the charge against me and why it was visited with the particular penalty which was imposed. Neither does any of the other eighteen priests who were parties to the case. We never had an opportunity to confront our accusers in any open forum, with the advice of counsel and in the presence of neutral third parties acting either as judge, conciliator, mediator or arbitrator.

For all of that, we were fortunate indeed. Not every priest involved in a similar case would have the assistance of a Committee of Concerned Canon Lawyers, or of a National Federation of Priests' Councils. The latter not only offered moral support, but also expended many thousands of dollars which we never could have afforded. It was because of these kinds of assistance that the case eventually reached Cardinal Wright.

Although much has been said in criticism of the publicity which attended the early phases of this experience, one has to wonder whether a less celebrated case would ever have reached the Congregation for the Clergy and the fair and impartial hearing which was finally given.

There is no assurance in the Church's present law that some obscure priest quietly trying to work himself out of the same dilemma, but without all the supports we had, would ever be able to make it.

If a case like ours were to occur today, Cardinal Wright, or someone else, would have to invent a process with which to solve it. And if there were no one who cared enough to invent a process, then it could never happen, because there is still no provision for it in the law of the Church.

Ours is a hierarchical Church, and among the people with whom I have been associated, none have ever denied the legitimate rôle, function, and authority of the members of the hierarchy. However, the manner in which the rôle and the authority are exercised may be largely the product of evolving human structures which can and should be changed in the light of new insights.

In an era when one of our most cherished insights has to do with the dignity of every human person, when much of the law of civilized nations is dedicated to the protection of the rights which go with that dignity, can the Church allow herself to be far behind?

Our whole Christian tradition answers the question for us. In cases where recourse is sought from the decision of a superior, especially where penalties have been imposed, there should be no long delay, no immense expenditure of money and energy over the course of many months, even years, no need for someone finally to invent a process to handle the matter.

The process should be there, written into the law, accessible and expeditious, and providing for a clear avenue to further appeal if this should become necessary.

I cannot see that provision for such guarantees would undermine hierarchical authority. There is no authority in the Church except that to which people willingly assent, motivated by their faith. The faith by which we Christians submit ourselves to authority demands a reciprocal response—a demonstrated faith that the authority which establishes guarantees for protecting human rights and dignity is opening the door, not to subversive alien creeds which could destroy it, but to the authentic voice of its own best traditions, that voice which has the Spirit as its source and guarantee.

# Contributors

JUAN LUIS ACEBAL, O.P., studied at Madrid and Salamanca. He is qualified in civil law, canon law and theology. He is Professor of Canon Law at the Pontifical University of Salamanca, Spain, and he has published in that field.

WILLIAM BASSETT has degrees in canon law (from the Gregorian) and civil law (from the Catholic University, Washington). He taught canon law at Washington and is now Professor of Law at the University of San Francisco. He has published many studies of canon law, civil law and legal history, and among his books is *The Bond of Marriage*.

JEAN BERNHARD is Professor of Canon Law at the University of Human Sciences at Strasbourg, France, and has been director of the Institute of Canon Law since 1970. He founded the review *Revue de Droit Canonique* which he still directs and in which he has published most of his studies of matrimonial law.

PIER GIOVANNI CARON holds degrees from Turin, Pavia and Milan. He is Professor in the History of State and Church Relations at Trieste University in the Faculty of Political Science. Among his works are a study of *Aequitas* and an analysis of the borderline between civil and ecclesiastical power.

ELIZABETH SCHÜSSLER-FIORENZA holds degrees from Würzburg and Münster, Germany, and is Professor in New Testament Studies at the University of Notre Dame, Indiana, USA. She has published on women in the Church, the priesthood, and apocalypse, and has recently edited a study of religious propaganda in Judaism and early Christianity.

THOMAS GREEN holds a doctorate from the Gregorian. Since 1972 he has been Chairman of the Canon Law Society Task Force on Revision of the Code. Since September 1974 he has been Assistant Professor of Canon Law at the Catholic University of America, Washington.

HANS HEIMERL studied at the University of Graz, Austria, and the Gregorian. From 1962 to 1972 he was Professor in Church Law at Graz and is now Reader at Linz University. Among his publications are studies of the functions of clergy and laity in the Church and a work on the laicized priest.

ENDA MCDONAGH is Professor of Moral Theology and Director of Post-graduate Studies, and Dean of the Faculty of Theology at St Patrick's College, Maynooth, Ireland. He is the author of works on Catholicism and unity, religious freedom, and various aspects of moral theology.

FRANCIS MORRISEY, O.M.I., holds degrees from Ottawa and Saint Paul University. He is Vice-Rector of Saint Paul University and Associate Professor and Dean of the Faculty of Canon Law. He is Editor of *Studia Canonica*. Among his many works are studies of canonical texts and of the canonical significance of papal and curial pronouncements.

JOHN NOONAN, Jr., is Professor of Law at the University of California, Berkeley. He has been a member of the Board of Governors of the Canon Law Society of America, and of the Due Process Committee of that society. He is the author of works on usury in scholastic thought, contraception, the power of dissolution and the individual and the law.

HARTMUT ZAPP is Privatdozent in Church Law and the History of Church Law at the University of Freiburg in Breisgau, Germany. Among his publications is a work on mental illness in the teaching on matrimonial consent of Thomas Sanchez.'